Chew With Your
Mouth Full

The Art of Feeding Your Face

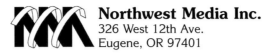

Northwest Media Inc.
326 West 12th Ave.
Eugene, OR 97401

ph: 800.777.6636 or 541.343.6636
email: nwm@northwestmedia.com

For online shopping and parent training go to: **www.SocialLearning.com**

Chew With Your Mouth Full
The Art of Feeding Your Face

By Diane Cissel

Illustrators

Cover: Dustin Dybevik

Other pages:

Diane Cissel
Eric DeBuhr
Dustin Dybevik
Carlos Gomez
Mike Novotny

Graphic Design

Diane Cissel

ISBN 1-892194-71-6

Table of Contents

Thanks to Anthony, Betty, Brigette, Carol, Caesar, Dustin,
Jennifer, Kris, Laurie, Lee, Marilyn, Mike, Scot, and Susan.
Your help and input made this book possible!

Introduction

Chew with Your Mouth Full helps you put together healthy, quick, low-cost meals with a minimum amount of effort and maximum success.

In this entertaining, tried and tested book, you'll find information on everything from outfitting a kitchen to making taste sensations like Renée's Chili Rellenos Casserole and Choco-Peanut Butter Candy.

Chew has 4 different menu plans. Each plan will keep a person well fed for a week. Everything is laid out - meals, snacks and desserts for every day, a shopping list for the entire week and a whole lot of recipes. Don't fret! If the cooking basics elude you - even how to boil water - you bought the right book. In this book, you'll learn how to do it all.

A lot of the food creations represented here come from *Getting Ready*, a life skills magazine for teens.

Chew is great for your stomach and easy on your mind. Oh, and please don't forget to chew with your mouth full!

Outfitting Your Kitchen

1. stove and conventional oven

2. blender

3. hand-mixer (either an electric one or a manual egg-beater)

4. optional: microwave oven

5. toaster or toaster oven

6. refrigerator

Basic Pots and Pans

GET YOUR KITCHEN GOING WITH THESE BASICS SO YOU CAN START COOKING RIGHT AWAY!

1. large cooking pot with a cover

2. large bowl for mixing stuff together

3. medium-size cooking pot

4. large frying pan

5. 9"x9" baking pan (metal or oven-safe glass)

6. 9"x13" baking pan (metal or oven safe glass)

More Pots and Pans

GET THESE OTHER POTS AND PANS WHEN YOU CAN. THEY'LL MAKE COOKING EASIER.

1. spaghetti strainer

2. 8" or 9" round cake pan

3. medium-sized frying pan

4. 2- to 3-quart oven-proof casserole dish

5. small cooking pot

6. baking sheet (a large metal pan with short sides)

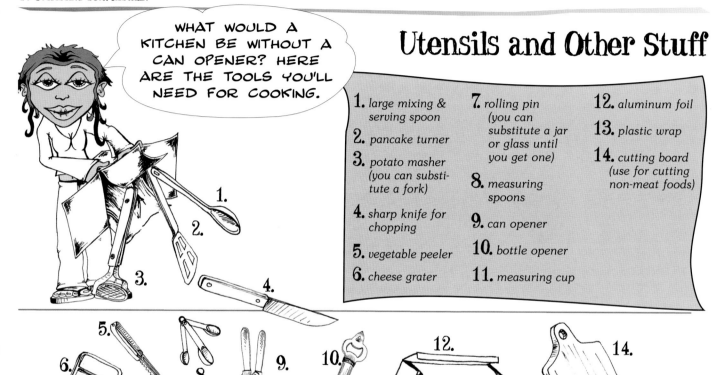

Utensils and Other Stuff

1. large mixing & serving spoon

2. pancake turner

3. potato masher (you can substitute a fork)

4. sharp knife for chopping

5. vegetable peeler

6. cheese grater

7. rolling pin (you can substitute a jar or glass until you get one)

8. measuring spoons

9. can opener

10. bottle opener

11. measuring cup

12. aluminum foil

13. plastic wrap

14. cutting board (use for cutting non-meat foods)

Four Weeks of Fabulous Feeds

Menu Plans and Shopping Lists

MENU PLANS?

YES! IF YOU PLAN WHAT YOU'RE GOING TO EAT FOR A WEEK, THEN YOU CAN BUY EVERYTHING YOU'LL NEED IN ONE SHOPPING TRIP AND SAVE TIME AND MONEY.

THIS CHAPTER GIVES YOU FOUR ONE-WEEK MENU PLANS AND THE SHOPPING LISTS TO GO WITH THEM.

I REALLY **LIKED** USING THE 12TH STREET MENU PLAN. THE RECIPES ARE REALLY **EASY**. NEXT WEEK I'M TRYING THE VEGETARIAN MENU PLAN.

ROASTED
POTATOES—
THUMBS UP!
(See Day 5)

This menu plan was kitchen-tested by Anthony.

Menu Plan User Guide

◉ You can make Day 1 stand for any day of the week.

◉ The complete shopping list to prepare all of the foods on this menu plan is on pages 14 & 15.

Day 1

Breakfast: Banana Pancakes (pg 72)
Lunch: Turkey sandwich
Snack: Fresh fruit
Dinner: Tuna Noodle Not-a-Casserole (pg 41) and Green Salad (pg 78), salad dressing

Day 2

Breakfast: Banana Smoothie (pg 96)
Lunch: Leftover Tuna Casserole
Snack: Carrot sticks with salad dressing dip, raisins
Dinner: Wraps (turkey, cheese, leftover Green Salad in a flour tortilla w/ salad dressing) (pg 42)
Dessert: Ice cream

Day 3

Breakfast: Cold cereal and/or toast, fruit juice
Lunch: Turkey sandwich with lettuce and tomatoes
Snack: Fresh fruit
Dinner: Spaghetti w/ meat sauce (pg 45), Green Beans & Almonds (pg 82)

Eat Meat Menu Plan

Day 4

Breakfast: Cold cereal and/or toast, fruit juice
Lunch: Peanut butter & jam sandwich *(pg 73)*, fresh fruit, carrot sticks
Snack: Crackers and cheese
Dinner: Baked Spaghetti with Cheese *(pg 45)* using leftovers from Day 3, leftover Green Beans & Almonds

Day 5

Breakfast: Oatmeal *(pg 36)* or other hot cereal, fruit juice
Lunch: Cheese sandwich
Snack: Fresh fruit
Dinner: Cheese Omelet *(pg 60)*, Roasted Potatoes *(pg 86)*, Carrot-Raisin Salad *(pg 79)*

Day 6

Breakfast: Banana Smoothie *(pg 96)*
Lunch: Leftover Carrot-Raisin Salad, peanut butter & jam sandwich *(pg 73)*
Snack: Fresh fruit
Dinner: Meatloaf *(pg 46)*, Roast Broccoli *(pg 93)*

Day 7

Breakfast: Scrambled Eggs *(pg 56)*, toast, and fruit juice
Lunch: Meatloaf sandwich *(pg 46)*
Snack: Crackers, fresh fruit
Dinner: Mojo Spuds *(pg 63)*, carrot sticks

Shopping Checklist for the Eat Meat Menu Plan

Shopping list facts

◉ Buying everything on this list will cost over $100. Check off the foods that you **already** have **before** you go to the store.

◉ This menu plan will cost about $10 per day—less if you always buy the cheapest brands. You'll also have food left over for next week.

◉ Foods under the same heading are usually in the same section of the grocery store.

DAIRY AND EGGS

- [ ] 1 dozen eggs
- [ ] 1/2 gallon milk or soy milk
- [ ] 1 8-oz container lowfat sour cream
- [ ] butter - *buy 1 lb at a time, but you'll need only 1/4 lb (1 stick) this week. It lasts a few weeks in the fridge.*
- [ ] 2 8-oz containers flavored yogurt
- [ ] 16 ozs cheddar cheese

PASTA & CANNED FOODS

- [ ] 12-oz can tuna
- [ ] 25-oz jar spaghetti sauce
- [ ] 12 ozs macaroni or spiral-shaped noodles
- [ ] 1 lb spaghetti noodles
- [ ] 14-oz can tomato sauce
- [ ] 1 container "seasoned" bread crumbs (or plain)
- [ ] 10-oz can condensed cream of mushroom soup

FRUITS & VEGETABLES

- [ ] 1 bunch leaf lettuce
- [ ] 1 cucumber
- [ ] 1 bunch radishes
- [ ] 3 or 4 carrots
- [ ] 1 green bell pepper
- [ ] 1 onion
- [ ] 1 head of broccoli
- [ ] 1 head of garlic
- [ ] 2 red potatoes
- [ ] 2 brown (baking) potatoes
- [ ] 3 bananas
- [ ] 6 fresh fruits (for example: apples, oranges, pears)

MEATS

- [ ] 3/4 lb sliced turkey
- [ ] 2 lbs ground beef

Shopping Checklist for the Eat Meat Menu Plan

SANDWICH & SNACK STUFF

- [ ] 1 dozen flour tortillas
- [ ] bread for sandwiches and toast (try whole wheat)
- [ ] peanut butter
- [ ] jam
- [ ] snack crackers
- [ ] mayonnaise
- [ ] salad dressing that you can also use as a dip
- [ ] 3-oz or 4-oz can of black or green olives, whichever you prefer (for salad)

BREAKFAST FOODS

- [ ] pancake mix
- [ ] cold breakfast cereal
- [ ] pancake syrup
- [ ] small jar of honey
- [ ] oatmeal (quick-cooking) or other hot cereal if you prefer
- [ ] 100% fruit juice (try orange or apple or pineapple), frozen or bottled

BAKING STUFF

- [ ] slivered almonds (about 1/4 cup)
- [ ] 15-oz box raisins
- [ ] brown sugar *(optional, for hot cereal)*
- [ ] 1 large bottle vegetable oil
- [ ] soy sauce

From the spice section:
- [ ] garlic powder
- [ ] chili powder
- [ ] salt and pepper

FROZEN FOODS

- [ ] 12 ozs frozen cut green beans
- [ ] 16 ozs frozen "French-cut" green beans
- [ ] pint of ice cream

What do the abbreviations mean?

◎ **oz = ounce**
◎ **lb = pound**

FRIED BANANAS TASTE REALLY GOOD WITH ROCKY ROAD ICE CREAM!
(See Day 6)

This menu plan was kitchen-tested by Kris.

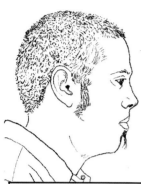

Menu Plan User Guide

◎ You can make Day 1 stand for any day of the week.

◎ The complete shopping list to prepare all of the foods on this menu plan is on pages 18 & 19.

Day 1

Breakfast: French Toast (pg 71), fruit juice
Lunch: Yogurt, Peanut Butter & Banana Wrap (pg 42)
Snack: Crackers and cheese
Dinner: Baked Noodles Ricotta (pg 55), Stir Fried broccoli, cauliflower, zucchini, green pepper (pg 92)

Day 2

Breakfast: English muffins and jam, fruit juice
Lunch: Leftover Noodles Ricotta
Snack: Apple, crackers
Dinner: Noodle Sauté with leftover Stir Fried Veggies and tuna fish (see "Other Tasty Additions" on pg 94)
Dessert: Pineapple Upside-down Cake (pg 106)

Day 3

Breakfast: Leftover Upside-down Cake, milk or soy milk
Lunch: Leftover Noodle Sauté, carrot sticks
Snack: Apple slices with peanut butter
Dinner: Lemony Chicken (pg 48), Spinach and Rice Bake (pg 77)

12th Street Menu Plan

Day 4

Breakfast: Oatmeal (pg 36) or other hot cereal, fruit juice
Lunch: Leftover Spinach Bake, chicken sandwich (use a few slices from leftover Lemony Chicken)
Snack: Leftover Upside-down Cake
Dinner: Chicken and Rice Casserole (pg 49), Green Bean Casserole (pg 84)

Day 5

Breakfast: English muffins and jam, fruit juice
Lunch: Yogurt, leftover Chicken and Rice Casserole
Snack: Raw cauliflower and carrots, w/ your favorite dressing or dip
Dinner: Fried Eggs (pg 58), Baked Acorn Squash (pg 89), leftover Green Bean Casserole

Day 6

Breakfast: Toast and jam or honey, fruit juice
Lunch: 2 English Muffin Pizzas (pg 74), leftover squash
Snack: Fresh fruit
Dinner: Pork Chops (pg 54), Roasted broccoli, cauliflower, zucchini, green pepper (pg 93)
Dessert: Fried Bananas w/ ice cream (pg 109)

Day 7

Breakfast: English muffins and jam
Lunch: Cheese sandwich with mayonnaise and mustard
Snack: Orange
Dinner: Spicy Chicken Wings (pg 50), leftover Green Bean Casserole

Shopping Checklist for the 12th Street Menu Plan

Shopping list facts

◎ Buying everything on this list will cost over $100. Check off the foods that you **already** have **before** you go to the store.

◎ This menu plan will cost about $10 per day—less if you always buy the cheapest brands. You'll also have food left over for next week.

◎ Foods under the same heading are usually in the same section of the grocery store.

DAIRY AND EGGS

- ☐ 1 dozen eggs
- ☐ 1/2 gallon milk or soy milk
- ☐ 16-oz container cottage cheese
- ☐ butter - *buy 1 lb at a time, but you'll need only 1/2 lb (2 sticks) this week. It lasts a few weeks in the fridge.*
- ☐ 2 8-oz containers flavored yogurt
- ☐ 8 ozs cheddar cheese
- ☐ 8-oz container grated parmesan cheese
- ☐ 8-oz container ricotta cheese

FROZEN FOODS

- ☐ 10-oz package frozen spinach
- ☐ 16-oz package "French-cut" green beans

FRUITS & VEGETABLES

- ☐ 2 lemons
- ☐ 3 onions
- ☐ 1 green bell pepper
- ☐ 1 stick of celery
- ☐ 1 large head of broccoli
- ☐ 1 head cauliflower
- ☐ 1 zucchini
- ☐ 1 acorn squash
- ☐ 1 banana
- ☐ 2 apples, and 2 other fresh fruits

What do the abbreviations mean?

◎ **oz = ounce**

◎ **lb = pound**

Shopping Checklist for the 12th Street Menu Plan

SANDWICH & SNACK STUFF

- [ ] snack crackers
- [ ] 1 dozen flour tortillas
- [ ] 1 loaf bread for sandwiches and toast
- [ ] 1 package English muffins
- [ ] peanut butter
- [ ] jam
- [ ] mayonnaise
- [ ] mustard (for sandwiches)
- [ ] salad dressing that you can use as a dip

BREAKFAST FOODS

- [ ] pancake syrup
- [ ] small jar of honey
- [ ] oatmeal (quick-cooking) or other hot cereal if you prefer
- [ ] 100% fruit juice (try orange or apple or pineapple), frozen or bottled

RICE & CANNED FOODS

- [ ] 12-oz can tuna
- [ ] 28-oz bag of white rice (long-grain)
- [ ] 14-oz can diced tomatoes
- [ ] 2 8-oz cans tomato sauce
- [ ] 1 can cream of mushroom soup
- [ ] 15-oz can pineapple pieces
- [ ] 5-oz bottle hot sauce
- [ ] 4-oz can mushrooms

BAKING STUFF

- [ ] white flour (at least 2 lbs)
- [ ] 2 llbs sugar
- [ ] brown sugar
- [ ] vanilla extract
- [ ] soy sauce
- [ ] 1 large bottle vegetable oil

From the spice section:

- [ ] garlic powder
- [ ] chili powder
- [ ] salt and pepper

MEATS

- [ ] 6 pieces chicken (can be any combination of thighs, breasts, and legs)
- [ ] 1 lb chicken wings
- [ ] 2 pork chops

I LOVE THE HUMMUS WRAPS!
(See Day 1)

This menu plan was kitchen-tested by Mike.

Menu Plan User Guide

◎ You can make Day 1 stand for any day of the week.

◎ The complete shopping list to prepare all of the foods on this menu plan is on pages 22 & 23.

Day 1

Breakfast: Oatmeal (pg 36) or other hot cereal, fruit juice

Lunch: Bagel sandwich with cream cheese, sprouts and/or lettuce and tomato

Snack: Carrot and cucumber slices w/ dip

Dinner: Hummus Wraps (pg 42)

Dessert: Peaches and Cream (pg 107)

Day 2

Breakfast: Toast and jam, cottage cheese (save some for another breakfast and 1/4 cup for the Twice-baked Potato on Day 6), orange juice

Lunch: Hummus and cream cheese on bagel, leftover Peaches and Cream

Snack: Fresh fruit

Dinner: Meat-free Chili (pg 62), Corn Bread (pg 97)

Day 3

Breakfast: Grilled leftover Corn Bread (pg 97), orange juice

Lunch: Hummus and cream cheese on bagel, carrot sticks

Snack: Rice cakes with peanut butter or cheese

Dinner: Crispy Burritos (pg 44) filled with left-over Meat-free Chili and cheese, Cucumber Salad (pg 80)

Vegetarian Menu Plan

Day 4

Breakfast: Grilled leftover Corn Bread *(pg 97)*, orange juice
Lunch: Cheese sandwich, leftover Cucumber Salad
Snack: Rice cakes with peanut butter or cheese
Dinner: Fettucine with Creamy Tomato Sauce *(pg 66)*, Orange-Black Bean Salad *(pg 81)*

Day 5

Breakfast: Orange Smoothie *(pg 96)*
Lunch: Leftover Fettucine and Black Bean Salad
Snack: Rice cakes with peanut butter or cheese
Dinner: Broccoli and Cheese Casserole *(pg 65)*, Baked Potatoes *(pg 85 - make 2, so you have 1 leftover for Day 6)*

Day 6

Breakfast: Toast and jam, cottage cheese *(save 1/4 cup for the Twice-baked Potato later today)*, fruit juice
Lunch: Leftover Broccoli Casserole
Snack: Rice cakes with peanut butter or cheese
Dinner: Twice-baked Potato *(pg 64 - use the leftover potato from Day 5)*, Baked Apple *(pg 95)*

Day 7

Breakfast: Bull's Eye Egg *(pg 61)*, grapefruit half
Lunch: Peanut Butter & Banana (or Jam) Sandwich *(pg 73)*
Snack: Grapefruit half leftover from breakfast, crackers
Dinner: Pizza with Ready-made Crust *(pg 67)*, Lemon Cauliflower *(pg 90)*
Dessert: Brownies *(pg 104)*

Shopping Checklist for the Vegetarian Menu Plan

Shopping list facts

◎ Buying everything on this list will cost over $100. Check off the foods that you **already** have **before** you go to the store.

◎ This menu plan will cost about $10 per day—less if you always buy the cheapest brands. You'll also have food left over for next week.

◎ Foods under the same heading are usually in the same section of the grocery store.

PASTA & CANNED FOODS

- [ ] 2 14-oz cans stewed tomatoes
- [ ] 1 28-oz can diced tomatoes
- [ ] 2 14-oz cans black beans
- [ ] 1 14-oz can kidney beans
- [ ] 1 15-oz can peaches
- [ ] 2 4-oz cans Anaheim or jalapeño chilies (you choose—jalapeños are hotter)
- [ ] 1 4-oz can mushrooms
- [ ] 1 package fettucine or spaghetti noodles (about 9 ozs)
- [ ] 1 8-oz can tomato sauce
- [ ] 1 16-oz can tomato sauce

BREAKFAST FOODS

- [ ] oatmeal (quick-cooking) or other hot cereal if you prefer
- [ ] 100% orange juice, frozen or bottled
- [ ] 1 package rice cakes or corn cakes
- [ ] small box raisins

FRUITS & VEGETABLES

- [ ] alfalfa sprouts (optional, for sandwiches)
- [ ] 1 bunch leaf lettuce for sandwiches
- [ ] 3 onions
- [ ] 2 brown (baking) potatoes
- [ ] 1 head garlic
- [ ] 1 small head cauliflower
- [ ] 3 green bell peppers
- [ ] 2 cucumbers
- [ ] carrots
- [ ] 1 grapefruit
- [ ] 2 oranges
- [ ] 1 lemon
- [ ] 3 bananas
- [ ] 2 apples
- [ ] 2 other fresh fruits for snacks

Shopping Checklist for the Vegetarian Menu Plan

SANDWICH & SNACK STUFF

- [ ] 3 bagels
- [ ] 1 dozen flour tortillas
- [ ] 1 loaf bread for sandwiches and toast
- [ ] peanut butter
- [ ] jam
- [ ] honey
- [ ] mayonnaise
- [ ] mustard
- [ ] smallest bottle balsamic vinegar
- [ ] salad dressing to use as dip
- [ ] 1 container hummus (garbanzo bean spread)
- [ ] 1 ready-made pizza crust
- [ ] 1 container or jar of salsa

DAIRY AND EGGS

- [ ] 1 dozen eggs
- [ ] 1/2 gallon milk or soy milk
- [ ] 16-oz container cottage cheese
- [ ] butter - *buy 1 lb at a time, but you'll need only about 3/4 lb (3 sticks) this week. It lasts a few weeks in the fridge.*
- [ ] 8-oz container plain yogurt
- [ ] 8-oz container vanilla yogurt
- [ ] 8 ozs cheddar cheese
- [ ] 8-oz package mozzarella cheese
- [ ] 4-oz package cream cheese
- [ ] 8-oz container grated parmesan cheese
- [ ] 12-oz package firm tofu
- [ ] whipped cream *(optional - to serve with the Peaches and Cream dessert)*

FROZEN FOODS

- [ ] 10-oz package frozen corn
- [ ] 2 16-oz packages frozen chopped broccoli

BAKING STUFF

- [ ] white flour
- [ ] corn meal (you'll need about a cup)
- [ ] smallest box baking mix (like Bisquick), about 40 ozs *(usually found near the flour)*
- [ ] baking powder
- [ ] sugar
- [ ] brown sugar *(optional, for hot cereal)*
- [ ] unsweetened cocoa
- [ ] 1 large bottle vegetable oil

From the spice section:
- [ ] chili powder
- [ ] cinnamon powder
- [ ] salt and pepper

CHILI RELLENOS CASSEROLE IS EVEN BETTER WHEN YOU ADD 1/2 TEASPOON CUMIN WITH THE FLOUR.

(See Day 3)

This menu plan was kitchen-tested by Scot.

Menu Plan User Guide

◉ You can make Day 1 stand for any day of the week.

◉ The complete shopping list to prepare all of the foods on this menu plan is on pages 14 & 15.

Day 1

Breakfast: Scrambled Eggs with Cheese and Veggies (pg 57), salsa
Lunch: Quesadillas (pg 98)
Snack: Canned fruit
Dinner: Baked Fish (pg 52), warm flour tortilla, Roasted Broccoli (pg 93)

Day 2

Breakfast: 2 Bagels and cream cheese, fruit juice
Lunch: Ham and Cheese Wrap (pg 42)
Snack: Canned fruit
Dinner: Skillet Dinner (pg 47) using leftover broccoli from Day 1

Day 3

Breakfast: Oatmeal (pg 36) or other hot cereal, fruit juice
Lunch: Ham sandwich with lettuce
Snack: Corn chips and salsa
Dinner: Renée's Chili Rellenos Casserole (pg 68), Refried Beans (pg 75)

Southwestern Style Menu Plan

Day 4

Breakfast: 2 Bagels and cream cheese, fruit juice
Lunch: Ham sandwich with lettuce and tomato
Snack: corn chips and salsa
Dinner: Flour tortillas filled with heated leftover Skillet Dinner and leftover Refried Beans, topped with salsa and cheese

Day 5

Breakfast: Oatmeal (pg 36) or other hot cereal, fruit juice
Lunch: Leftover Chili Rellenos Casserole
Snack: Apple
Dinner: Black Beans and Rice (pg 69), salsa, warm flour tortilla

Day 6

Breakfast: 2 Bagels and cream cheese, fruit juice
Lunch: Wrap (pg 42) with leftover Beans and Rice and salsa
Snack: Banana and peanut butter
Dinner: Rice Verde (pg 76), Artichoke (pg 91)
Dessert: Apple Crisp (pg 108)

Day 7

Breakfast: Bull's Eye Egg (pg 61)
Lunch: Leftover Rice Verde, carrot sticks
Snack: Leftover Apple Crisp
Dinner: BBQ Baked Chicken (pg 51), Roasted Broccoli (pg 93)

Shopping Checklist for the Southwestern Style Menu Plan

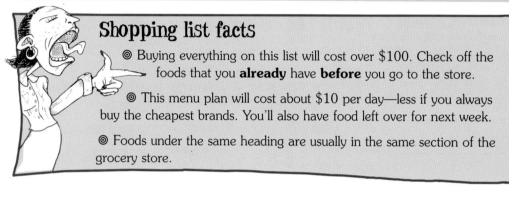

Shopping list facts

◎ Buying everything on this list will cost over $100. Check off the foods that you **already** have **before** you go to the store.

◎ This menu plan will cost about $10 per day—less if you always buy the cheapest brands. You'll also have food left over for next week.

◎ Foods under the same heading are usually in the same section of the grocery store.

DAIRY AND EGGS

- ☐ 1 dozen eggs
- ☐ 1/2 gallon milk or soy milk
- ☐ butter - *buy 1 lb at a time, but you'll need only about 1/2 lb (2 sticks) this week. It lasts a few weeks in the fridge.*
- ☐ 1 lb cheddar cheese
- ☐ 16-oz container lowfat sour cream

MEATS

- ☐ 1 lb ground beef
- ☐ 1/2 lb fish fillets
- ☐ 1/2 lb sliced ham
- ☐ 4 chicken pieces (legs or thighs)

FRUITS & VEGETABLES

- ☐ 1 bunch leaf lettuce for sandwiches
- ☐ 2 lemons
- ☐ 2 onions
- ☐ celery
- ☐ green bell pepper
- ☐ 1 head of broccoli
- ☐ 1 artichoke
- ☐ carrots
- ☐ 5 apples
- ☐ 1 banana

What do the abbreviations mean?

◎ **oz = ounce**
◎ **lb = pound**

Shopping Checklist for the Southwestern Style Menu Plan

SANDWICH & SNACK STUFF

- [ ] 1 dozen flour tortillas
- [ ] 1 loaf bread for sandwiches and toast
- [ ] 6 bagels
- [ ] peanut butter
- [ ] mayonnaise
- [ ] mustard (for sandwiches)
- [ ] 12-oz bottle barbecue sauce
- [ ] 16-oz container fresh salsa, bottled salsa or taco sauce
- [ ] corn chips

BREAKFAST FOODS

- [ ] small jar of honey
- [ ] oatmeal (quick-cooking)
- [ ] 100% fruit juice (try orange or apple or pineapple), frozen or bottled

RICE & CANNED FOODS

- [ ] 1 28-oz bag white rice (long-grain)
- [ ] 2 15-oz cans fruit, like peaches or apricots
- [ ] 2 7-oz cans whole green chilies
- [ ] 2 4-oz cans chopped jalapeño or anaheim chilies (you choose—the jalapeños are hotter)
- [ ] 2 14-oz cans pinto beans
- [ ] 1 14-oz can black beans
- [ ] 1 14-oz can stewed tomatoes
- [ ] 3 ozs to 4 ozs black or green olives

BAKING STUFF

- [ ] 2 lbs white flour
- [ ] 2 lbs sugar
- [ ] small bag brown sugar
- [ ] 1 large bottle vegetable oil
- [ ] soy sauce

From the spice section:
- [ ] garlic powder
- [ ] chili powder
- [ ] dill
- [ ] cumin
- [ ] cinnamon
- [ ] salt and pepper

The Basics

HERE'S THE ABC'S OF COOKING. YOU NEED THESE SKILLS TO GET STARTED.

How to Boil Water

1 Put the desired amount of water into a pot. Be sure the pot is big enough so the water doesn't reach the very top. Allow about 2" from the top of the pot so the bubbling, boiling water stays inside.

2 Place the pot on the stove, cover and turn the heat up to high. This is the time to add salt to the water if the recipe calls for it.

3 The water is boiling when there are bubbles coming to the surface continually.

Boiling Water Facts:

Add Salt
If you add salt to the water, it boils a little faster.

What Does "Simmer" Mean?
"Simmer" means to slow down the boil by lowering the heat, and then cooking over the lowered heat. Simmering water has smaller bubbles than boiling water.

To Cover or Not to Cover
Putting a cover on the pot while the water is heating will speed up the boiling. When you add the food to the boiling water, take the cover off to prevent boiling over.

How to Cook Noodles

1 Fill a large pot with water to about 2" from the top. Add 1 teaspoon salt. Bring to a boil over high heat.

2 While you're waiting for the water to boil, measure out the amount of noodles you'll need according to your recipe.

3 When the water boils, add noodles and stir. When the water boils again, turn down the heat to one notch below high. Noodles will boil over if you don't turn down the heat to cook them.

4 Cook noodles for the amount of time listed on their package, or until they are soft enough to eat but not mushy. You can test them by carefully removing a noodle with a spoon, running it under cold water to cool, and tasting it.

5 When noodles are done they need to be drained. The easiest way is to put a spaghetti strainer in the sink and pour the whole pot into the strainer. You can also use the pot cover to hold back the noodles while you carefully pour off the water into the sink, but sometimes you lose noodles by doing this.

6 As noodles cool they stick together, so either use them in your recipe right away, or stir in a couple teaspoons of vegetable oil to coat them.

Here's a sample of the many faces of noodles

Macaroni   Fusilli   Flat Egg Noodles   Manicotti

How to Cook Long-grain Rice

(makes 2 cups cooked rice)

ingredients
- 1 cup white long-grain rice or white long-grain basmati rice
- 2 cups water
- 1/2 teaspoon salt
- 2 teaspoons vegetable oil

1 In a medium-sized pot that has a cover, combine the water, salt, and oil.

2 Cover the pot and bring the water to a boil.

3 Add the rice and immediately turn heat down to medium low. Put the cover back on and cook over low heat for about 20 minutes, or until all the water is absorbed into the rice.

You can test to see if it's done by gently pushing a spoon down to the bottom of the pot and moving some rice aside to see if all the water is gone yet.

NOTE: If you are cooking **brown** long grain rice, increase the the water to 2 1/4 cups and increase the cooking time over low heat to 40-45 minutes.

Intro to Chopping Vegetables

There are so many ways to chop and so many different vegetables. Here are some examples.

Onion

Chop off the ends of the onion.

Peel off the skin.

Slice it in half.

Slice it this way for long thin pieces or....

Slice it this way and then...this way for chunky shapes.

Pepper

Chop the pepper lengthwise.

NOTE: *If you chop a hot chili pepper, wash your hands to remove the irritating chili oils.*

In each half you'll find lots of little white seeds. Break off the stem with your hands, and scrape out the seeds.

Slice each half lengthwise into strips.

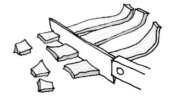

Slice the strips into small chunks.

Broccoli

Chop off the bottom 1"-2" of the stalk.

Chop 1/4" pieces off the stalk.

Chop until you get to the base of the "flowerettes" near the top.

Cut off the flowerettes at their base, then just chop up whatever is left of the stalk.

Basic Oatmeal

(1 serving)

ingredients
1 cup water
1/2 teaspoon salt
1/2 cup quick-cooking oatmeal
Toppings (optional) such as a little butter and brown sugar
or syrup or jam or honey

1 Put 1 cup water and 1/2 teaspoon salt in a small or medium-sized pot. Bring to boil over high heat.

2 Stir in 1/2 cup oatmeal. Turn heat down to medium and cook, while stirring, until thick (about 1-2 minutes).

3 Serve with any toppings listed above, if you like.

Words and Measurements

Beat - To make a mixture smooth by quickly stirring it (with some muscle behind it) with a spoon, fork, or other utensil.

Boil - To cook in boiling water.

Broil - To cook food directly under the heat source.

Cream - To beat butter or other shortening with sugar or honey until completely smooth and creamy.

Cut In - To quickly work butter or other shortening into the dry ingredients so the shortening becomes small pieces.

Dice - To cut into small cubes.

Fold In - To mix gently with a spoon or rubber spatula from the bottom of the bowl to the top. This keeps as much air as possible in the mixture.

Grease - To coat a baking dish with a thin layer of oil or shortening.

Julienne - To cut into long thin strips.

Leavening - Ingredients that make baked goods rise, like baking powder or yeast.

Marinate - To let food soak in a liquid mixture called a marinade. It's for adding flavor to the food.

Mince - To cut into tiny pieces (smaller than diced).

Pare - To peel or trim vegetables and fruit.

Purée *(pronounced "pyer-ray")* - To blenderize or mash a food into a thick liquid.

Roast - To cook uncovered in the oven.

Roux *(pronounced "roo")* - A cooked paste of equal parts butter or oil and flour. Used to thicken sauces.

Sauté *(pronounced "saw-tay")* - To cook food in a frying pan with a small amount of oil while stirring.

Scald - To cook a liquid until just before it boils.

Shortening - The fat added to baked items, like butter or vegetable shortening.

Simmer - To cook food in a liquid at a low enough temperature that only small bubbles break the surface.

Toss - To thoroughly combine several ingredients by mixing gently.

Whip - To beat quickly with a whisk, egg beater or electric mixer to add air to the ingredients. It makes egg whites and cream light and fluffy.

Whisk - To mix quickly with a utensil, called a whisk, that has looped wires on the end. If a recipe says to whisk in an ingredient, you can probably substitute a fork.

Measurements

3 teaspoons = 1 tablespoon
4 tablespoons = 1/4 cup
2 tablespoons = 1 fluid ounce
2 cups = 1 pint
4 cups = 1 quart
2 pints = 1 quart
4 quarts = 1 gallon
1 cube butter = 1/2 cup

Recipes

Recipes are divided into three sections:

◎ **Main Dishes.** This section is also divided
into **Meat** and **Vegetarian** dishes.

◎ **Small Meals and Side Dishes.**

◎ **Desserts.**

Main Dishes *with meat*

Tuna Noodle Not-a-Casserole

ingredients
8 ozs uncooked corkscrew-shaped noodles or macaroni
1 12-oz package frozen cut green beans
1 10-oz can condensed cream of mushroom soup
1 cup milk
1 cup shredded mozzarella cheese
1 12-oz can tuna with liquid drained off
Salt and pepper

1 Cook noodles according to package directions, drain off the water when done.

2 While the noodles cook, put the green beans into a large pot and cover them with water. Add 1/2 teaspoon salt. Bring them to a boil over high heat, turn heat down to medium-high, and cook 15 minutes. Drain off the water.

3 Add the soup, milk, mozzarella cheese, tuna, and noodles to the green beans. Mix together well. Add about 1/8 teaspoon of pepper, mix again.

4 Put pot on medium heat. Cook and stir until cheese melts and it's heated through. Serve immediately.

 This recipe is included in the Eat Meat Menu Plan (pg 12-13)

Wraps

These creations can be anything you want. You can use leftovers, hot or cold.

ingredients

1 large flour tortilla

Something spreadable such as cream cheese, mayonnaise, hummus (garbanzo bean spread), cottage cheese, etc.

Meat and/or cheese

Vegetables such as lettuce, grated carrots, sliced cucumbers or pickles, or leftover cooked vegetables

Salad dressing, salsa, or other sauce

1 Lay out flour tortilla.

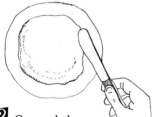

2 Spread the "something spreadable" to 1 inch from the outer edge of the tortilla.

3 Lay out the meat and/or cheese in a rectangle a couple of inches from the side edges.

4 Put the rest of the ingredients on top of the meat/cheese layer. Top with salad dressing, salsa, or other sauce.

 This recipe is included in the Vegetarian Menu Plan (pg 20-21)

...Rolling Up Wraps

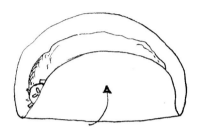

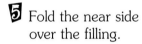 **5** Fold the near side over the filling.

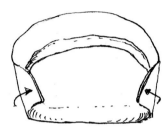 **6** Fold in the sides.

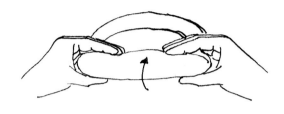 **7** Roll over towards the top. You can keep an extra-full tortilla together by wrapping in aluminum foil or waxed paper.

8 Finished.

 **9** Eat it up.

Crispy Burritos

You can fill these with leftovers like chili or refried beans.

ingredients

2 burrito-size flour tortillas, or
3 regular-size flour tortillas

1/2 cup grated cheddar cheese

1/4 cup salsa

2 tablespoons sour cream or plain
yogurt

Your choice of the following (you'll need
about 2/3 cup total):
- leftover refried beans
- leftover chili
- black beans
- pieces of cooked chicken, pork, or beef

1 tablespoon vegetable oil or butter

1 Lay a tortilla out flat. Put about 1/3 cup of your choice filling (the refried beans, chili, etc.) in a rectangle a couple of inches from the side edges.

2 Spoon on half the salsa and half the sour cream or yogurt. Place half the cheese over the top.

3 Fold up Wrap-style (see previous page) and leave seam-side down to keep it together.

4 Put the oil or butter into a frying pan big enough to hold 2-3 burritos. Turn heat to medium, and let the butter or oil heat up for a minute.

5 Place the burritos seam-side down in the pan, cover and let cook for 2-3 minutes, or until the burritos are lightly browned. Check often because they burn easily. When first side is browned, turn over with a pancake turner, cover the pan, and cook the other side for a few minutes. When browned, remove from heat and serve.

 This recipe is included in the Vegetarian Menu Plan (pg 20-21)

Spaghetti with Meat Sauce

ingredients

25-oz jar spaghetti sauce

1/2 cup water

1 onion, chopped up

1 green or red bell pepper, chopped

2 tablespoons vegetable oil

1 lb ground beef

1 lb spaghetti noodles

1 Put oil in a large pot and turn the heat to medium. Add chopped onion and bell pepper and cook for 5 minutes.

2 Add ground beef, turn the heat up to medium-high. Cook and stir until beef is no longer pink.

3 Stir in jar of spaghetti sauce and 1/2 cup water. Turn the heat down to medium and cook for 30 minutes.

4 While the sauce cooks, make the noodles according to the directions on the package. Drain noodles and serve with the sauce.

Leftovers I

Keep the sauce and noodles separate so the noodles don't get soggy. You can keep the sauce in the fridge for 3-4 days, or in the freezer for 2-3 months. *From www.FoodSafety.gov*

Leftovers II - Baked Spaghetti with Cheese

- Mix the noodles and sauce together.
- Pour them into a baking pan, top with grated cheddar cheese.
- Bake in the oven at 350 degrees for 30 minutes.

 This recipe is included in the Eat Meat Menu Plan (pg 12-13)

Meatloaf

ingredients for meatloaf:

1 lb ground beef

1/2 teaspoon salt

1/4 teaspoon pepper

1 teaspoon garlic powder

1 large egg

1/2 cup bread crumbs

1/2 cup from a 14-oz can of tomato sauce

1 teaspoon soy sauce

ingredients for sauce:

The rest of the 14-oz can of tomato sauce

2 tablespoons brown sugar

1 teaspoon soy sauce

1 Combine all ingredients for the meatloaf by using your clean hands to squish it all together.

2 Form into a large oval loaf.

3 Place in a 9"x13" pan, bake at 350° for 45 minutes.

4 While the meatloaf bakes, make the sauce: Combine all ingredients in a saucepan, cook over medium heat for 5-10 minutes.

5 Pour the sauce over the meatloaf and serve.

What do you do with leftover meatloaf?

Store it in the refrigerator and use it up in the next few days:

◎ Slice it for sandwiches—tasty with ketchup.

◎ Crumble it for a Wrap or Crispy Burrito filling (pages 42 & 44).

◎ Slice it and heat it in a microwave. Dip chunks in ketchup, mustard, or creamy salad dressing.

This recipe is included in the Eat Meat Menu Plan (pg 12-13)

Skillet Dinner

Everything for your meal in one big simple dish.

ingredients

1 lb gound beef

1 tablespoon vegetable oil

1 onion, chopped

2 sticks celery, chopped

1 red or green bell pepper, chopped

1 cup broccoli, cut into bite-sized chunks, or leftover cooked broccoli

2 teaspoons chili powder

1 14-oz can stewed tomatoes

2 cups cooked rice (see page 33)

1 Cook rice according to package directions (or see page 33).

2 While the rice cooks, add 1 tablespoon oil to a large frying pan. Turn the heat to medium and add the chopped onion, bell pepper, and celery. Cook until onion is soft (about 5-10 minutes).

3 Add the ground beef to the frying pan and turn the heat up to medium-high. Stir and cook until the ground beef has no pink left in it. (Better check that rice!)

4 Stir the chili powder, broccoli pieces, and stewed tomatoes into the meat mixture .

5 Turn heat down to medium, put a cover on the pan and cook for 15 minutes, or until broccoli is soft. **Note:** *if you use leftover cooked broccoli, you can skip this step.*

6 Stir in the cooked rice and serve.

 This recipe is included in the Southwestern Style Menu Plan (pg .24-25)

Lemony Chicken

ingredients

6 pieces chicken (any combination of thighs and legs)

1 lemon

2 tablespoons vegetable oil

1/2 teaspoon salt

1 teaspoon garlic powder (or more if you love garlic)

Pepper

1 Squeeze the juice out of the lemon into a small bowl. Remove the seeds. Combine the juice with the oil, salt, garlic powder, and some pepper.

2 Place the chicken pieces skin side up in a single layer in a 9"x13" pan. Put 1 teaspoon of the lemon juice mixture under the skin of each piece by forcing the spoon up under the skin. Pour any leftover lemon juice mixture evenly over the top of all the chicken pieces.

3 Bake at 375° for 45 minutes, or until chicken is lightly browned on top.

Leftovers

If you have leftover chicken, pull the meat off the bones and store it in the refrigerator. Use it in 1 or 2 days for tasty sandwiches, or for the Chicken and Rice Casserole on the next page.

 This recipe is included in the 12th Street Menu Plan (pg 16-17)

Chicken and Rice Casserole

This is a great way to use leftover cooked chicken.

ingredients

1 cup uncooked rice

1 4-oz can mushrooms

1 cup chopped, cooked chicken
(you can use leftover chicken)

2 tablespoons mayonnaise

1/2 cup milk

1 tablespoon vegetable oil

1 onion

1 green or red bell pepper

1/2 cup shredded cheddar cheese

1 Cook rice according to package directions *(or see page 33)*.

2 Chop the onion and bell pepper.

3 Put the oil into a frying pan and turn heat to medium. Add the chopped onion and bell pepper and cook for 5-10 minutes, until soft.

4 In a mixing bowl, combine the cooked onion and pepper with mushrooms, chicken chunks, mayonnaise, milk, and shredded cheese.

5 Place the cooked rice in a casserole dish or a 9"x13" pan. Pour the chicken mixture over the rice. Bake uncovered at 350° for 25 minutes.

 This recipe is included in the 12th Street Menu Plan (pg 16-17)

Spicy Chicken Wings

ingredients

1 lb chicken wings

1 5-oz bottle hot sauce

1/2 teaspoon brown sugar

1/2 teaspoon butter

1 Cut the wings apart at the joints. Throw away the tips (the pointy pieces).

2 Spread the wings out on a baking sheet. Bake them in the oven at 325° for 20 minutes (or until they are well-browned).

3 Remove the wings from the oven and let cool for 5 minutes.

4 While they cool, mix together in a saucepan the hot sauce, brown sugar, and butter. Heat and stir over low heat (don't let it boil, or it doesn't taste as good). When the butter melts and the sauce is warm, remove the pan from the stove.

5 Pour the sauce over the wings in the pan and mix around to coat all the wings with sauce. Let soak for 20 minutes and serve.

This recipe is included in the 12th Street Menu Plan (pg 16-17)

BBQ Baked Chicken

ingredients

4 chicken pieces (legs or thighs)

1 tablespoon vegetable oil

1/4 cup barbecue sauce from a bottle

1 Preheat oven to 350°.

2 Cut skin off from the chicken. Place chicken in a baking pan and rub a little vegetable oil onto each piece.

3 Sprinkle each piece all over with salt and pepper.

4 Bake for 35 minutes in the oven.

5 Remove pan from oven, spread barbecue sauce on each piece and return to oven. Turn heat up to 400° and bake for 10-15 minutes.

Leftovers

Take the meat off the bone, put it in a bowl, and store it in the refrigerator for up to 3 days. Use it for sandwiches, Wraps (page 42), or Crispy Burritos (page 44).

 This recipe is included in the Southwestern Style Menu Plan (pg 24-25)

Baked Fish

This recipe serves one. Use about 1/2 pound (which is 8 ounces) of fish per person.

ingredients

1/2 lb fish fillets like flounder, red snapper, cod, or sole

1 tablespoon butter

1/2 teaspoon dried dill (from the spice section of the grocery store)

1 1/2 teaspoons soy sauce

Salt and pepper

1 In a small saucepan, melt the butter over low heat (so it doesn't burn). Mix in dill and soy sauce.

2 Place fish in a baking dish. Spoon butter mixture evenly over fish.

3 Cover with aluminum foil and bake at 400° for 15 minutes, or until fish falls apart easily when poked with a fork.

This recipe is included in the Southwestern Style Menu Plan (pg 24-25)

Be adventurous

Experiment with spices you haven't tried before. Smell a new spice and then try to imagine it with the taste of fish. Some good ones for fish include Chili Powder, Garlic, and Paprika.

Tuna Salad

ingredients
- 1 12-oz can tuna
- 2 tablespoons mayonnaise
- 1 stick of celery
- 1/2 teaspoon pepper

1 Chop the celery.

2 Drain the water from the can of tuna. Put tuna into a mixing bowl.

3 Combine the tuna, mayonnaise, celery, and pepper. Mix well.

Favorite ways to eat Tuna Salad

Put it in a sandwich with lettuce.

Mix it with fresh tomatoes and serve it with cottage cheese on the side.

Use it as a Wrap filling (*see page 42*) with salsa and cheese.

 This recipe is included in the 12th Street Menu Plan (pg 16-17)

Pork Chops

This recipe also makes a sauce that you can put over rice or noodles.

ingredients
2 pork chops
Salt and pepper
1 tablespoon vegetable oil
1 14-oz can diced tomatoes

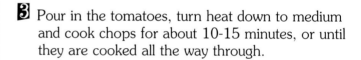 **NOTE** If you want to eat just **1 pork chop**, wrap one in plastic and freeze it for up to 4 months. Defrost it in the fridge. To prevent spoilage, never re-freeze meat.

1 Sprinkle both sides of pork chops with salt and pepper.

2 Put a large frying pan over medium high heat and add the oil. Add pork chops and brown on both sides for about a minute.

3 Pour in the tomatoes, turn heat down to medium and cook chops for about 10-15 minutes, or until they are cooked all the way through.

 This recipe is included in the 12th Street Menu Plan (pg 16-17)

Buying Pork Chops

The types of pork chops you can buy are named according to which part of the pig the meat came from. Pork Loin Chops and Pork Rib Chops both work for this recipe.

Baked Noodles Ricotta

ingredients

2 cups uncooked flat egg noodles	1/4 teaspoon garlic powder
2 tablespoons vegetable oil	1/4 teaspoon salt
1 cup ricotta cheese	pepper
2 eggs, beaten	1/2 cup grated parmesan cheese

1 Cook the noodles according to the package directions, making sure not to cook them too long or they'll become mushy.

2 In a mixing bowl combine the cooked noodles with the rest of the ingredients.

3 Rub oil on the bottom and sides of a 9"x9" baking dish. Place the noodle mixture in the pan. Bake at 350° for 30 minutes, or until hot and bubbly.

 This recipe is included in the 12th Street Menu Plan (pg 16-17)

Scrambled Eggs

ingredients

2 eggs

2 tablespoons milk

Sprinkling of salt and pepper

2 teaspoons vegetable oil

THERE'S LOTSA PROTEIN IN THEM EGGS.

1 In a bowl combine the eggs, milk, salt, and pepper. Beat with a fork until well-mixed.

2 Put the vegetable oil in a medium-sized frying pan and spread it around with a pancake turner. Turn heat to medium. The pan is hot enough when a drop of water sizzles when you drop it in.

3 Pour in the egg mixture. Using a pancake turner, swirl the eggs and scrape the cooked portions off the pan until all the eggs are solid. Cook them to the hardness you like—the longer you cook them, the harder and drier the eggs will be.

This recipe is included in the Eat Meat Menu Plan (pg 12-13)

Scrambled Eggs with Cheese and Veggies

ingredients

2 eggs

Chunk of cheese (as much as you
    want to eat for this meal), cut into
    small pieces

2 tablespoons milk

sprinkling of salt and pepper

1/4 of an onion, chopped

1/4 of a bell pepper, chopped

2 teaspoons vegetable oil

1 In a bowl combine the eggs, cheese, milk, salt and pepper. Beat with a fork until well-mixed.

2 Put the vegetable oil in a medium-sized frying pan and spread it around with a pancake turner. Turn heat to medium. Add the onion and bell pepper and cook until the onion is soft.

3 Pour in the egg mixture. Using a pancake turner, swirl the eggs and scrape the cooked portions off the pan until all the eggs are solid. Cook them to the hardness you like—the longer you cook them, the harder and drier the eggs will be.

NOTE See page 34 for information about chopping onions and bell peppers.

 This recipe is included in the Southwestern Style Menu Plan (pg 24-25)

Fried Eggs

ingredients

2 eggs

2 teaspoons vegetable oil

1 teaspoon water

1 Put oil into a frying pan and spread it around with a pancake turner. Turn heat to medium. The pan is hot enough when a drop of water sizzles when you drop it in.

2 Carefully break each egg right into the pan, trying not to break the yolks. Reduce heat to low and cook until the edges turn white.

WHAT'S THE BEST SPORT FOR AN EGG YOLK?

RUNNING!

3 Add the water and cover the pan. Cook to desired firmness (2-3 minutes). Serve immediately.

NOTE It's possible to get sick from Salmonella bacteria in eggs, but here's how you can reduce the risk:

Keep eggs in the refrigerator until you use them.

Throw out cracked or dirty eggs.

Eats eggs right after cooking them—don't keep them at room temperature for more than 2 hours.

Don't eat raw eggs.

From the Centers for Disease Control and Prevention (www.cdc.gov).

Soft-cooked or Hard-cooked Eggs

Soft-cooked eggs have a solid white part and a runny yolk, hard-cooked eggs have a solid white and a solid yolk.

ingredients

2 eggs

Water

The first 2 steps are the same for hard- and soft-cooked eggs

1 Put eggs in small pot. Fill pot with enough water to reach about 1 inch over the eggs.

2 Cook over high heat until boiling.

Then, for a soft-cooked egg:

▪ Let boil for 1 minute. Remove from heat.

▪ Cover pot with lid and let stand for about 3 minutes.

▪ Remove lid, remove eggs with spoon to a small bowl.

▪ Run cold water over eggs for about 1 minute, or until eggs are cool enough to handle.

Or, for a hard-cooked egg:

▪ Let eggs boil for 10 minutes. Remove from heat.

▪ Remove eggs with spoon to a small bowl.

▪ Run cold water over eggs for about 2 minutes, or until eggs are cool enough to handle.

IF YOU CAN'T TELL THE RAW EGGS FROM THE HARD-COOKED EGGS IN THE FRIDGE, DO THE SPIN TEST: SPIN AN EGG ON A FLAT SURFACE. IF IT SPINS SMOOTHLY IT'S HARD-COOKED, BUT IF IT WOBBLES A LITTLE IT'S RAW.

Cheese Omelet

ingredients

4 eggs	1/8 teaspoon pepper
2 tablespoons water	2 teaspoons vegetable oil
1/2 teaspoon salt	1/4 cup grated cheese (like cheddar, monterey jack, or swiss)

1 In a bowl combine the eggs, water, salt, and pepper. Beat with a fork until well-mixed.

2 Put the vegetable oil in a medium-sized frying pan and spread it around with a pancake turner. Turn heat to medium. The pan is hot enough when a drop of water sizzles when you drop it in.

3 Pour in the egg mixture. As the eggs cook for the first minute, gently lift the edges so the uncooked part flows underneath. Put the cover on the pan and cook over medium heat for another 3 minutes, or until the eggs look like they're getting solid.

4 Sprinkle the cheese over the eggs, and fold the omelette in half using a pancake turner. Cook another 30 seconds, then lift it out and serve on a plate.

 This recipe is included in the Eat Meat Menu Plan (pg 12-13)

Bull's Eye Egg

ingredients

1 egg

1 slice of bread

2 teaspoons butter

1 Rip a hole in the center of the bread, about the size of an egg yolk. Eat the little circle of bread you removed now, or fry it with the bread and egg to eat later.

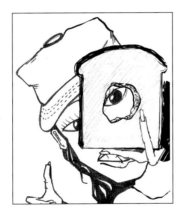

2 Melt the butter in a frying pan over medium heat and spread it around with a pancake turner. Add the bread and cook on 1 side until browned. Turn the bread over with a pancake turner.

3 Break the egg into the hole and cook 2-3 minutes. Flip over with the pancake turner and cook another 1 minute, or until the clear part of the egg turns white.

 This recipe is included in the Vegetarian Menu Plan (pg 20-21)

Meat-free Chili

ingredients

1 14-oz can black beans

1 14-oz can kidney beans

2 4-oz cans chopped jalapeño or anaheim chilies (jalapeños are hotter than anaheims)

1 red or green bell pepper

3 cloves of garlic, with the papery skin peeled off

1 onion

1 28-oz can diced tomatoes

1 14-oz can stewed tomatoes

2 tablespoons vegetable oil

1 tablespoon balsamic vinegar *(see page 81 to find out about this special vinegar)*

1 tablespoon chili powder

1 Chop the onion, bell pepper, and garlic into small pieces.

2 Put 2 tablespoons oil in a large pot. Turn heat to medium and add the onion, bell pepper, and garlic. Cook until onion is soft.

3 Stir in the rest of the ingredients. Turn heat up to high and bring to a boil. As soon as it boils, turn heat down to medium and cook for 30 minutes.

Leftovers

Store chili in a covered bowl in the refrigerator for 1-4 days. Here are 2 tasty ideas:

◎ Heat it up in a pot, spoon some onto a burrito, top with grated cheese and roll it up.

◎ Spoon some heated chili over the top of a Cheese Omelet *(page 60)* before serving.

 This recipe is included in the Vegetarian Menu Plan (pg 20-21)

Mojo Spuds

ingredients

2 medium-sized potatoes

2 tablespoons butter

2 tablespoons sour cream

1/2 teaspoon chili powder

Salt and pepper

1 Preheat oven to 375°.

2 Wash the potatoes well.

3 Prick each potato several times with a fork (this lets steam escape when you cook them, so they won't burst open in your oven).

4 Place potatoes on a baking pan and bake in the oven for about 45 minutes, or until a fork can easily be inserted into a potato.

5 Remove potatoes, let cool for about 2 minutes. Cut each potato in half lengthwise (so they make long boat shapes). Scoop out the potatoes with a spoon and put the insides in a bowl—save the potato skins. Add the remaining ingredients and mash together well. Re-fill the hollowed out potato skins and serve.

Or microwave the potatoes

◎ Prick each potato several times with a fork. Arrange potatoes at least 1 inch apart in the microwave.

◎ Microwave potatoes on HIGH for 4 minutes.

◎ Turn potatoes over.

◎ Microwave for 4 more minutes on HIGH.

This recipe is included in the Eat Meat Menu Plan (pg 12-13)

Twice-baked Potato

ingredients

1 russet potato (the large brown potatoes)

2 teaspoons mayonnaise

1 tablespoon plain yogurt

1/4 cup cottage cheese

1/4 cup grated cheddar cheese

1 teaspoon mustard

Salt and pepper

1 Prick the potato with a fork and bake it in the regular oven or the microwave oven (see page 63). *If using a leftover baked potato, start at #2.*

2 Let the potato cool for 5-10 minutes. Cut potato in half the long way. Scoop out the insides, making boat shapes out of the 2 halves.

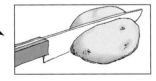

3 Put the insides in a large mixing bowl and mash well with a fork. Add the remaining ingredients and mix well.

4 Arrange the potato skins side by side in a baking pan. Fill each skin with the potato mixture. Bake at 350° for 30 minutes, or until the tops of the potatoes begin to brown.

 This recipe is included in the Vegetarian Menu Plan (pg 20-21)

Broccoli and Cheese Casserole

ingredients

2 16-oz packages frozen chopped broccoli

1/2 cup grated cheddar cheese

1 onion

1 4-oz can mushrooms with liquid drained off

2 tablespoons vegetable oil

1/2 cup milk

2 eggs

1/2 teaspoon salt

Pepper

1 Cook broccoli according to package directions. Drain and set aside.

2 Chop onion into small pieces.

3 Put the oil in a frying pan. Turn heat to medium, add onion pieces and cook until they are soft.

4 In a large mixing bowl, beat the eggs to break up the yolks. Add the milk, cheese, broccoli, onion pieces, mushrooms (with liquid drained off), salt and some pepper. Mix well and pour into a 2- to 3-quart casserole dish (a 9"x13" baking pan will also work).

5 Bake at 350° for 45 minutes *(if you are making this as part of the Vegetarian Menu Plan, bake the casserole for 30 to 40 minutes at the same temperature as the potatoes—375°).*

 This recipe is included in the Vegetarian Menu Plan (pg 20-21)

Fettucine with Creamy Tomato Sauce

ingredients

6 ozs firm tofu

2 tablespoons vegetable oil

1/2 teaspoon salt

Half an onion

1 16-oz jar spaghetti sauce

1/4 cup milk

1 package fettucine (or you can substitute spaghetti noodles), about 9 ozs

Grated parmesan cheese

1 Cut the tofu into bite-sized squares. Chop the onion into small pieces.

2 Cook fettucine or spaghetti according to package directions (*or see page 32*). When noodles are done, drain them and place in a large serving bowl.

3 While noodles cook, put the oil into a medium-sized pot, turn heat to medium-high. Heat for 1 minute. Add tofu pieces and salt. Cook for 5-10 minutes, scraping bottom of pot with a pancake turner to keep tofu from sticking.

4 Remove tofu to a small bowl and set aside. Reduce heat to medium and add the onion pieces. Cook until the onion is soft.

5 Add the tomato sauce to the pot. Stir, then scrape the bottom of the pot so nothing is left sticking to it.

6 Remove the sauce from heat and add the milk. Stir well. Gently stir in the cooked tofu pieces.

7 Pour sauce over noodles in the bowl, sprinkle with parmesan cheese and serve.

 This recipe is included in the Vegetarian Menu Plan (pg 20-21)

Pizza with Ready-made Crust

ingredients

1 ready-made pizza crust

1 teaspoon vegetable oil

1 8-oz can tomato sauce

8 ozs mozzarella cheese, grated

Your choice of pizza toppings

1 Spread the oil on the crust.

2 Spread on about 1/4 cup tomato sauce.

3 Sprinkle the mozzarella cheese on top of the sauce. Place whichever toppings you choose all over the pizza.

4 Bake at 450° for 10 minutes, or until cheese is bubbly.

PSST... HERE'S SOME GOOD STUFF TO PUT ON YOUR PIZZA.

sliced olives

chopped red or green bell pepper

sliced mushrooms

chopped onions

sliced pepperoni

pesto sauce (this topping goes directly on the dough before you put on the sauce)

chopped anchovies (anchovies are salty little fish!)

This recipe is included in the Vegetarian Menu Plan (pg 20-21)

Renée's Chili Rellenos Casserole

ingredients

2 7-oz cans whole green chilies (remove seeds and open flat)

10 ozs cheddar cheese, grated

2 eggs

2 tablespoons flour

1/2 teaspon cumin

Your favorite fresh or canned salsa to serve with the meal

1 Heat oven to 350°.

2 Put one layer of chilies on the bottom of a 9"x9" baking pan (use 1 can).

3 Sprinkle on cheese, and place the rest of the chilies on top.

4 Beat the eggs, flour, and cumin together in a small bowl. Pour on top of the casserole.

5 Bake for 30 minutes.

6 Serve with salsa.

This recipe is included in the Southwestern Style Menu Plan (pg 24-25)

Black Beans and Rice

ingredients

1 cup uncooked rice

1 tablespoon vegetable oil

1 14-oz can black beans

Juice from 1/2 of a lemon or lime (about 1 1/2 tablespoons)

2 teaspoons chili powder

1/2 teaspoon salt

Your favorite fresh or canned salsa to serve with the meal

Sour cream to serve with the meal

1 Cook rice according to package directions *(or see page 33).*

2 Put oil in a large frying pan. Turn heat to medium. Pour in the the beans and cook for 5 minutes. While the beans cook, mash them with a fork or potato masher until most of the beans are crushed.

3 Add the lemon or lime juice, chili powder and salt. Cook until it starts to bubble.

4 Serve with cooked rice, salsa and sour cream.

THERE ARE MORE BEAN RECIPES IN THE SIDE DISHES SECTION.

 This recipe is included in the Southwestern Style Menu Plan (pg 24-25)

Macaroni and Cheese Casserole

ingredients

8 ozs elbow macaroni

10 ozs cheddar cheese, grated

1/2 cup milk

1 Cook macaroni noodles according to the package directions *(or see page 32)*. Drain well when done.

2 Put half the noodles into a 2- to 3-quart casserole dish. Sprinkle half the cheese on top. Add the rest of the noodles, then add the rest of the cheese.

3 Pour milk evenly over the casserole.

4 Bake at 350° for 30 minutes or until cheese is melted and slightly browned.

YOU CAN MAKE THIS RECIPE EVEN BETTER:

◎ COOK I CUP OF YOUR FAVORITE CHOPPED FROZEN VEGETABLES ACCORDING TO THE PACKAGE DIRECTIONS.

◎ DRAIN WELL.

◎ MIX THE VEGGIES WITH THE COOKED NOODLES IN STEP I, THEN DO THE REST OF THE STEPS.

French Toast

ingredients

1 egg

2 tablespoons milk

2 slices bread

1 tablespoon vegetable oil

Your choice of toppings such as:
- pancake syrup
- honey
- butter
- jam
- cinnamon sugar (this is a mixture of 1 teaspoon cinnamon and 3 tablespoons sugar)

1 Beat the egg and milk together in a shallow dish.

2 Put the oil into a frying pan. Turn heat to medium.

3 Dip each slice of bread in the egg mixture and place in frying pan.

4 Cook until brown on one side, then turn over and cook until brown on the other side. Serve with your choice of toppings.

I LIKE TO MAKE MY FRENCH TOAST WITH SOURDOUGH BREAD.

This recipe is included in the 12th Street Menu Plan (pg 16-17)

Banana Pancakes

ingredients

1 banana

1/2 cup whole wheat flour

1 cup white flour

1/2 teaspoon salt

1 teaspoon baking powder

1 egg

1 cup milk

Vegetable oil for frying

Pancake topping such as pancake
syrup, jam, honey, or cinnamon sugar

1 Cut banana into small pieces (bean-sized). Put into a small bowl and set aside.

2 Mix flours, salt, and baking powder together in a large mixing bowl.

3 Beat the milk and egg together with a fork.

4 Combine the flour mixture and the egg mixture. Mix well, so no lumps are left.

5 Put about 1 teaspoon vegetable oil in a frying pan and turn heat to medium. When you put a drop of water in the pan and it sizzles, then the pan is hot enough for frying the pancakes.

6 Drop a large spoonful of batter onto the hot pan. Sprinkle with the little pieces of banana. Cook the pancake for a few minutes, until the edges start to become solid. Turn the pancake over with a pancake turner and cook for another few minutes, until cooked through and lightly browned.

7 Repeat steps 5 and 6 until all the batter is used up. Serve with a pancake topping.

 This recipe is included in the Eat Meat Menu Plan (pg 12-13)

Small Meals and Side Dishes

Peanut Butter and _____ *(fill in the blank)* Sandwich

Peanut butter can be combined with a lot of different ingredients to make tasty, nutritious sandwiches. Here's how to make the best peanut butter sandwich:

1 Lay out 2 slices of bread and spread peanut butter on both halves.

2 On top of the peanut butter add your favorite topping such as:

OR POTATO CHIPS AND PICKLE SLICES. IT'S GOOD.

jam

HONEY

sliced banana

thin slices of apple or strawberries

CHEDDAR CHEESE

grapes

celery slices

English Muffin Pizza

ingredients

1 English muffin

2 tablespoons canned tomato sauce

2 slices of mozzarella cheese or cheddar cheese

2 tablespoons each of chopped vegetables of your choice, such as red or green bell pepper, mushrooms, onion, or olives

1 Separate the English muffin into 2 halves. Toast the halves on the light toaster setting. Put them on a plate.

2 On each half spread 1 tablespoon tomato sauce. Top each with 1 slice of cheese and 1 tablespoon of each of the vegetables you chose.

3 Place the muffin halves on a baking sheet and place in the oven on a rack near the top. Turn oven to broil and cook for only a few minutes to melt the cheese. It browns quickly on the broil setting. *NOTE: Most ovens require that you leave the oven door open a little on the broil setting.*

When the cheese is melted it is ready to eat.

You can also broil the English muffins in a toaster oven to melt the cheese.

 This recipe is included in the 12th Street Menu Plan (pg 16-17)

Refried Beans

ingredients

2 14-oz cans pinto beans

2 teaspoons chili powder

1/2 teaspoon garlic powder

1/2 teaspoon cumin

2 teaspoons lemon juice

Salt and pepper to taste

1 1/2 tablespoons vegetable oil

1 Pour beans into a mixing bowl and mash them until they are smooth. Add the chili powder, garlic, cumin, salt, pepper. Mix well.

2 Put the oil into a frying pan and turn the heat to medium high. Add the beans and cook until they are bubbly. Stir in the lemon juice and serve.

How to eat those leftover beans...

First, heat them up in a pot on the stove or in a bowl in the microwave, then:

◉ Sprinkle them with 1/4 cup shredded cheese and eat them with rice.

◉ Roll them in a flour tortilla with sour cream and salsa.

◉ Dip corn chips in them (serve with salsa).

 This recipe is included in the Southwestern Style Menu Plan (pg 24-25)

Rice Verde

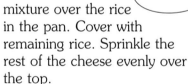

"VERDE" (PRONOUNCED <<VAIR-DAY>>) MEANS "GREEN" IN SPANISH.

ingredients

1 cup uncooked long-grain rice

1/2 teaspoon butter

1/3 cup light (lowfat) sour cream

1 4-oz can chopped green chilies

1/2 cup grated cheddar or monterey jack cheese

EEWWWW, I'M NOT GONNA EAT GREEN RICE.

1 Cook rice according to package directions *(or see page 33)*.

2 Smear butter on the inside of a 9"x9" baking pan.

3 Place half the rice into the pan.

4 In a mixing bowl, combine sour cream, chilies, and half the cheese. Spread this mixture over the rice in the pan. Cover with remaining rice. Sprinkle the rest of the cheese evenly over the top.

5 Bake at 350° for 25 minutes.

BUT IT TASTES GOOD.

This recipe is included in the Southwestern Style Menu Plan (pg 24-25)

Spinach and Rice Bake

ingredients

1 cup uncooked rice

1 10-oz package frozen spinach

1 onion

1 tablespoon vegetable oil

1 4-oz can mushrooms

1 16-oz container cottage cheese

1/4 cup milk

1 egg

1 teaspoon garlic powder

1/4 cup shredded cheddar cheese

1/2 teaspoon salt, 1/2 teaspoon pepper

1/2 teaspoon chili powder

1 Cook the rice according to package directions *(or see page 33)*.

2 Fill a pot halfway with water. Add 1 teaspoon salt. Bring to a boil over high heat.

3 Add spinach and cook until it separates and is no longer frozen. Drain and set aside.

4 Chop the onion into small pieces. Put the oil in a frying pan and turn the heat to medium high. Add the onion and cook until it is soft.

5 In a mixing bowl combine the mushrooms, ricotta cheese, milk, egg, garlic, cheese, salt, pepper, chili powder, onions, spinach, and rice.

6 Pour into a 2-quart casserole dish. Bake covered for 30 minutes at 350°.

 This recipe is included in the 12th Street Menu Plan (pg 16-17)

Green Salad

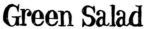

ingredients

1 head of leafy lettuce

Some combination of:
tomato
cucumber
radish
can of sliced olives
green or red bell pepper

1 Tear off the whole leaves of lettuce and wash under cold water. Shake the water off the leaves, tear each one into bite-sized pieces, and put into a large bowl.

2 Wash the rest of the ingredients that you've chosen. Chop them into bite-sized pieces, add them to the lettuce, and toss it all together. Serve with your favorite dressing.

If you're feeling adventurous, try these tasty bits in your salad:

◎ Walnuts
◎ Apple pieces
◎ Raisins or dried cranberries
◎ Small chunks of cheese, like cheddar or feta
◎ Pieces of fresh, raw green beans or snow peas

 This recipe is included in the Eat Meat Menu Plan (pg 12-13)

Carrot-Raisin Salad

SUCH A SIMPLE SALAD!

ingredients

2 medium-sized carrots
2 tablespoons raisins
1 tablespoon mayonnaise

1 Wash and peel the carrots. Grate them into a mixing bowl.

2 Add the raisins.

3 Add the mayonnaise and mix well.

 This recipe is included in the Eat Meat Menu Plan (pg 12-13)

Cucumber Salad

ANOTHER SIMPLE SALAD!

ingredients

1 cucumber
1 1/2 teaspoons vinegar
1/2 teaspoon salt

1 Wash cucumber in cold water. Peel off the skin.

2 Slice into very thin pieces and put in a bowl.

3 Mix in the vinegar and the salt. Let sit 10 minutes, then serve.

THIS ONE'S AS EASY TO MAKE AS THE CARROT-RAISIN SALAD ON PAGE 79!

This recipe is included in the Vegetarian Menu Plan (pg 20-21)

Orange-Black Bean Salad

ingredients

1 14-oz can black beans

1 10-oz package frozen corn

1 red or green bell pepper

1 tablespoon vegetable oil

2 tablespoons balsamic vinegar (or 2 tablespoons white vinegar and 1/2 teaspoon brown sugar)

1 orange

1 teaspoon chili powder

1 Empty package of corn into a medium-sized pot and cover with water. Turn heat to high and bring water to a boil. Turn heat down so it doesn't boil over, and cook until corn is hot and no longer frozen (about 5 minutes).

2 Chop bell pepper into small pieces.

3 Cut the orange in half and squeeze out the juice into a bowl. Remove any seeds from the juice.

4 Open the can of beans and drain off the liquid.

This recipe is included in the Vegetarian Menu Plan (pg 20-21)

Pour into a mixing bowl and add the cooked corn, bell pepper, oil, vinegar, orange juice, and chili powder. Mix well and refrigerate until cool. This salad tastes even better the next day.

What IS Balsamic Vinegar?

Balsamic vinegar is dark brown and tastes sour and slightly sweet because it's made from grapes. Other vinegars don't taste sweet. You can find it in the grocery store near the regular vinegar. The cheapest brand will taste great in this recipe.

Green Beans & Almonds

ingredients

1 16-oz package "French-cut" green beans

2 tablespoons butter

1/4 cup chopped almonds *(you can find chopped almonds in the baking section of the grocery store, or buy them whole and chop them yourself)*

1 Place almonds on a baking sheet in a single layer. Place on top rack of oven and turn heat to broil. Leave in for just a few minutes until the almonds begin to brown. Watch out—they burn easily! Remove from oven and set aside.

2 Empty package of green beans into a pot. Add enough water to just cover the green beans. Cook over high heat until the water boils.

3 Turn heat down to medium and cook for 15 minutes, or until beans are a duller green. Drain the water off.

4 While green beans cook, melt the butter in a microwave for 20 seconds, or in a small pot over low heat.

5 Place cooked and drained green beans in a bowl, drizzle with butter and add almonds. Mix and serve.

 This recipe is included in the Eat Meat Menu Plan (pg 12-13)

Soy-sautéed Green Beans

ingredients

1 16-oz package frozen "French-cut" green beans

1/2 onion

2 teaspoons vegetable oil

2 teaspoons soy sauce

1 Empty package of green beans into a pot. Add enough water to just cover the green beans. Cook over high heat until the water boils.

2 Turn heat down to medium and cook for 15 minutes, or until beans are a duller green. Drain the water off.

3 While the beans cook, slice the onion into thin slices *(see page 34)*. Put the oil in a frying pan and turn the heat to medium. Add the onion and cook until it is soft.

4 Add the soy sauce to the pan and stir it in. Add the cooked green beans and turn heat up to medium high. Cook for 3 minutes, mixing with a pancake turner to keep them from burning and sticking to the pan.

Classic Green Bean Casserole

ingredients

1 16-oz package "French-cut" green beans

2/3 cup milk

1/2 can cream of mushroom soup

1/2 onion

1/4 teaspoon pepper

1 Empty package of green beans into a pot. Add enough water to just cover the green beans. Cook over high heat until the water boils.

2 Turn heat down to medium and cook for 15 minutes, or until beans are a duller green. Drain the water off.

3 While beans cook, chop onion into thin slices (see page 34).

4 In a mixing bowl, combine mushroom soup, pepper, and milk. Mix well. Stir in the cooked green beans.

5 Pour into 2- to 3-quart casserole dish. Spread onion slices evenly on top. Bake uncovered at 350° for 30 minutes.

 This recipe is included in the 12th Street Menu Plan (pg 16-17)

Simple Baked Potatoes

If you have one of these leftover, you can make a Twice-baked Potato *(page 64)*.

ingredients

2 russet (baking) potatoes

Optional additions:
    salt and pepper
    butter
    sour cream

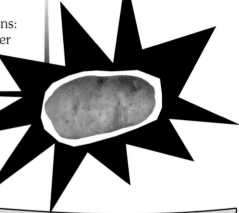

1 Preheat oven to 375°.

2 Wash potatoes well.

3 Prick the potatoes several times with a fork. This lets steam escape when you cook them, so they won't burst open in your oven.

4 Place potatoes on a baking pan and bake in the oven for about 45 minutes, or until a fork can easily be inserted into the potatoes.

5 Remove from the oven, let cool 10 minutes, and serve with salt and pepper, butter or sour cream.

This recipe is included in the Vegetarian Menu Plan (pg 20-21)

Or microwave your potatoes

◎ Prick the potatoes several times with a fork. Arrange potatoes at least 1 inch apart in the microwave.

◎ Microwave potatoes on HIGH for 4 minutes.

◎ Turn potatoes over.

◎ Microwave for 4 more minutes on HIGH.

Roasted Potatoes

ingredients

3 red potatoes

4 teaspoons vegetable oil

1/4 teaspoon salt

1/4 teaspoon chili powder

1 Preheat oven to 425°.

2 Wash potatoes and cut them into wedges *(see below)*. Place them in a mixing bowl.

3 Pour on the oil and mix well. Add the salt and chili powder and mix to coat the potatoes evenly.

4 Spread potatoes out in a single layer on a baking sheet.

5 Place pan in 425° oven and bake for 15 minutes, then scrape the potatoes off the bottom of the pan using a pancake turner. Place baking sheet back into oven and bake for 15 minutes more, stir with a pancake turner, and bake 5-10 minutes more, or until potatoes are browned and soft enough to insert a fork easily.

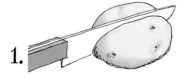

1.

2. wedge

This recipe is included in the 12th Street Menu Plan (pg 16-17)

Mashed Potatoes

ingredients

4 russet (baking) potatoes

1 teaspoon salt (for cooking water)

1/4 cup milk

Salt and pepper

OPTIONAL: 4 cloves of garlic to make Garlic Mashed Potatoes

1 Wash and peel potatoes. Cut them into large chunks.

2 Place potatoes (and garlic cloves if you are adding them) in a large pot, add 1 teaspoon salt and enough water to cover potatoes.

3 Cook potatoes over high heat until the water boils, lower the heat to medium-high and cook for 15-20 minutes, or until potatoes are soft enough to mash. Check them with a fork.

4 When they're done, drain off the water. Mash potatoes (and garlic) with a potato masher or large fork until lumps are gone.

5 Add 1/4 cup milk and mix until smooth. Mix in more milk if you want them less stiff. Mix in about 1/4 teaspoon salt and some pepper.

What to do with that pile of leftover mashed potatoes:

◎ Make Potato Pancakes (page 88). Eat them with Fried Eggs (page 58) or just some salt and pepper.

◎ Use them for a filling in Crispy Burritos (page 44).

Potato Pancakes

You need leftover mashed potatoes to make these.

---

ingredients

Leftover mashed potatoes
2 tablespoons vegetable oil

---

1 Scoop up a small handful of mashed potatoes (about 3 tablespoons), and make a small hamburger shape. Place on a plate. Repeat with rest of potatoes.

2 Put 2 tablespoons of vegetable oil in a frying pan. Turn heat to medium high and let frying pan heat up for a minute. Put the potato pancakes in the hot pan, about an inch apart.

3 Cook pancakes for 3-4 minutes, or until browned. Turn them over with a pancake turner to cook the other side. They'll stick to the pan, so you have to carefully scrape underneath the cakes as you turn them. Cook another 3 minutes until browned on second side. Remove from the pan and serve.

4 If you have more than 1 batch, repeat steps 2 and 3.

This recipe is included in the Eat Meat Menu Plan (pg 12-13)

Baked Acorn Squash

ingredients

1 acorn squash	1 tablepoon butter
Salt	2 teaspoons brown sugar

1 Cut squash in half lengthwise (from stem to bottom). Use a spoon to scoop and scrape out seeds. Sprinkle each half with salt.

2 Arrange squash cut-side up in a shallow baking pan. Cover each half tightly with aluminum foil.

3 Bake at 350° for 1 hour. Remove aluminum foil covers.

4 Put 1/2 tablespoon butter and 1 teaspoon brown sugar in each squash half.

5 Return pan to the oven and bake without a cover for 10 minutes, or until you can easily insert a fork through the skin. Serve with the skin, but eat just the orange part by scooping it out with a spoon.

NO, THIS ISN'T A PUMPKIN, IT'S AN ACORN SQUASH. IT'S DARK GREEN WITH ORANGE SPLOTCHES ON THE OUTSIDE AND ALL ORANGE ON THE INSIDE.

This recipe is included in the 12th Street Menu Plan (pg 16-17)

Lemon Cauliflower

ingredients

1 head cauliflower

1 tablespoon juice from a lemon

1/2 teaspoon salt

1 Cut out the center stem of the cauliflower. Break the rest apart into "flowerettes"–each flowerette looks like a little white tree.

2 Place in a pot and add about 1 inch water. Turn heat to high and bring to a boil. Turn heat down to medium and cover pot. Cook 15 minutes, or until cauliflower pieces are soft enough for a fork to be inserted easily.

3 Drain off water. Cut open the lemon and squeeze out 1 tablespoon of the juice. Mix juice with the salt. Pour over the cauliflower and mix to coat it. Serve and add salt and pepper to taste.

You probably won't finish that whole head of cauliflower...

Make a salad with the leftovers:

◉ Put the leftovers in a bowl and pour 3 tablespoons of your favorite non-creamy dressing (like italian) over it. Mix gently to coat cauliflower. Store in the fridge for up to a week.

 This recipe is included in the Vegetarian Menu Plan (pg 20-21)

Artichoke

ingredients

1 artichoke

2 tablespoons butter

2 teaspoons lemon juice

1 Wash artichoke in water. Pull off lower petals which are small or discolored.

2 Cut stem off close to base.

3 Put artichoke stem side down into a medium pot and fill with enough water to reach about 1 inch over the artichoke. Turn heat to high and bring water to a boil. Turn heat to medium high and boil for 45 minutes. Remove from water.

4 Melt the butter, either for 20 seconds in a microwave, or in a small pot on low on the stove. Mix in the lemon juice.

How to eat an artichoke

◎ Tear off a leaf.

◎ Dip it in the lemon butter.

◎ Use your teeth to scrape off the soft part of the leaf. The leaves get softer as you get closer to the middle. After you're finished with the leaves, there is a part that looks hairy – scrape off and discard this part to get to the artichoke heart (the most tender part of the artichoke).

This recipe is included in the Southwestern Style Menu Plan (pg 24-25)

Stir-fried Veggies

I LIKE 'EM STIR FRIED!

ingredients

2 tablespoons vegetable oil

Salt and pepper

1 teaspoon chili powder or
2 teaspoons soy sauce

Any combination of these vegetables:

- broccoli
- cauliflower
- red or green bell pepper
- onion
- zucchini
- celery
- bok choy (it's like celery)

1 Chop vegetables into bite-sized chunks.

2 Put the oil in a frying pan and turn heat to medium. Add onion pieces and cook until onion is soft.

3 Add other vegetable chunks and turn heat up to medium-high.

4 Cook for 5-7 minutes, mixing with a pancake turner to keep vegetables from burning and sticking to the pan (this is called sautéing – pronounced "saw-tay-ing").

5 Add the soy sauce, mix in, and keep sautéing until the vegetables are cooked as much as you want. The longer you cook them, the softer they'll become.

This recipe is included in the 12th Street Menu Plan (pg 16-17)

I LIKE 'EM ROASTED!

Roasted Veggies

ingredients

2 tablespoons vegetable oil

Salt and pepper

1 teaspoon chili powder (optional)

3 cups vegetables chopped into bite-sized chunks. Use a combination such as these:

- broccoli
- cauliflower
- onion
- zucchini
- sweet potato or yam

1 Preheat oven to 400°. *If you need to set the oven to 375° or 350° for a food you're baking at the same time, increase the baking time for the veggies.*

2 Place chopped vegetables in a mixing bowl.

3 Add the oil and mix to coat all the vegetables. Add salt (and chili powder, if you want it)

and mix to coat the vegetables. Spread them on a baking sheet in a single layer.

4 Bake at 400° for 15 minutes, or until the vegetables are barely beginning to brown. *Bake at 375° for 20 minutes or 350° for 25 minutes.*

Too many veggies?

Use leftover roasted or stir-fried veggies in the Noodle Sauté on the next page.

This recipe is included in the 12th Street Menu Plan (p.16) and the Eat Meat Menu Plan (pg 12-13)

Noodle Sauté with Leftover Vegetables

Cook up some Roasted Veggies (page 93) if you don't have any leftovers.

ingredients

4-6-ozs noodles (spaghetti, spiral, or macaroni)

1 tablespoon vegetable oil

Leftover cooked vegetables (such as zucchini, broccoli, cauliflower, onions, bell peppers, or green beans)

3 tablespoons parmesan cheese

1 Cook the noodles according to the package directions *(or see page 32)*.

2 Put the oil in a frying pan and turn heat to medium. Add leftover vegetables and cook until they are heated through. Add the noodles and mix them in. Cook until everything is hot.

3 Put noodle mixture in a bowl, sprinkle on the parmesan cheese and serve.

 This recipe is included in the 12th Street Menu Plan (pg 16-17)

Other tasty additions:

◎ Drain the water off a 12-oz can of tuna, and add it right after the leftover veggies.

◎ If you like anchovies, chop some up in tiny pieces and cook them in the frying pan for a minute before adding the vegetables.

◎ Add sliced black olives with the cheese (you can buy them already sliced in a can).

Baked Apples

ingredients

2 apples

2 tablespoons raisins

1/4 cup orange juice

1/2 teaspoon ground cinnamon

1 Wash the apples in water and peel them. Cut them in half and remove the *core*—the seeds and the hard parts around them.

Coring apples:

Cut an apple in half.

Use a knife to cut out the seeds and the surrounding hard part.

A hollow well is left where the core was.

2 Put the orange juice in a bowl. Dip the apples in orange juice to coat them.

3 Place the apples, flat-side up, on a baking dish. Put 1/4 of the raisins in each well left by the removed apple cores. Pour a teaspoon of orange juice over the raisins. Sprinkle with cinnamon.

4 Bake at 350° for 25 minutes. Serve hot or cold.

 This recipe is included in the Vegetarian Menu Plan (pg 20-21)

SMOOTHIES!

You need a blender for these recipes.

Banana Smoothie

ingredients

1 cup milk
8-oz container yogurt (vanilla or a
   berry flavor)
1 banana

1 Put the milk into the blender. Add the yogurt. Break the banana into pieces and add to the blender.

2 Put the top on and blend until smooth (about 30 seconds).

Orange Smoothie

ingredients

1 cup orange juice
1 banana
1 8-oz container vanilla yogurt
3 ice cubes
1 teaspoon honey

1 Put orange juice, yogurt, ice cubes, and honey in a blender. Break the banana into pieces and add to blender.

2 Put the top on and blend until smooth (about 30 seconds).

This recipe is included in the Eat Meat Menu Plan (pg 12-13) *and* the Vegetarian Menu Plan (pg 20-21)

Corn Bread

ingredients

3/4 cup corn meal

1 cup flour

2 teaspoons baking powder

3/4 teaspoon salt

1 egg

1/4 cup milk

1 cup plain (not sweetened) yogurt

2 tablespoons vegetable oil

2 tablespoons honey

Vegetable oil to grease baking pan

1 Preheat oven to 425°.

2 In a large mixing bowl combine the corn meal, flour, baking powder, and salt.

3 In another bowl mix together the egg, milk, yogurt, oil, and honey.

4 Add the egg mixture to the flour mixture and mix well.

5 Smear the oil on the inside of a 9"x9" pan. Pour in the batter.

6 Bake at 425° for 20 minutes, or until the edges of the bread are just starting to turn a light brown. Cut into squares and serve.

Grilled Corn Bread

◎ Slice a piece of corn bread in half.

◎ Heat a frying pan over medium heat. Add 1 teaspoon vegetable oil or butter.

◎ Add the pieces of corn bread and fry until browned, about 3-4 minutes.

 This recipe is included in the Vegetarian Menu Plan (pg 20-21)

Quesadillas (pronounced kay-sah-dee-yas)

> **ingredients**
> 2 flour tortillas
> 1/3 cup grated cheddar cheese
> 1 teaspoon vegetable oil
> Salsa to serve with them

1 Spread out 1 tortilla and sprinkle 3 tablespoons cheese on half of it. Fold tortilla in half over cheese. Repeat with other tortilla.

2 Put oil in a frying pan and turn heat to medium.

3 Add the folded tortillas and cook for 3-5 minutes, until lightly browned. Turn tortillas and cook on second side for 3-5 minutes until browned.

4 Place quesadillas on a plate and cut into triangles. Serve with salsa.

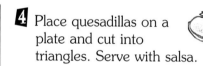

Tasty additions to quesadillas

Sprinkle any or all of these over the cheese before folding the tortilla:
- ◎ Sliced olives from a can
- ◎ Diced anaheim or jalepeño peppers from a can
- ◎ Pieces of avocado
- ◎ Pieces of tomato

This recipe is included in the Southwestern Style Menu Plan (pg 24-25)

Grilled Cheese and Green Chilies

ingredients

1-2 tablespoons butter, softened to room temperature *(to soften, either leave the butter, covered, at room temperature for 1/2 hour, or heat it in a microwave for about 5 seconds)*

1 4-oz can chopped green chilies

2 slices whole wheat bread

Cheese (cheddar is good)

1 Open the can of chilies and drain off the liquid.

2 Place slices of cheese on 1 piece of bread—enough to cover the whole piece.

3 Scatter 1 tablespoon chilies over the cheese. Use the leftover chopped chilies in another meal.

4 Put the second piece of bread on top and spread the top and bottom of the sandwich with butter.

5 Heat frying pan over low heat for 2 minutes.

6 Cook the sandwich on one side until browned, flip over and cook the other side until brown and the cheese is melted.

Black-eyed Peas

Let these soak overnight before you cook them for 3 hours the next day.

---

ingredients

2 cups dried black-eyed peas

4 strips of bacon

Water

---

1 Rinse peas in a strainer. Put them into a bowl and cover with water. Cover bowl and let peas soak at room temperature overnight.

2 The next day, drain off the water and put the peas into a large cookpot. Add enough water so it comes to about 2 inches above the peas.

3 Add the bacon strips and bring the water to a boil over high heat. When it starts to boil, turn the heat down to medium-low so the water just simmers.

4 Simmer the peas slowly, adding water if the level gets down as far as the peas. Cook for 3 hours or until the peas are soft.

Taste-bud pleasing additions

◎ After 2 hours of cooking, add to the pot:
- 1/2 chopped onion
- 2 stalks chopped celery
- 1 16-oz can diced tomatoes

Cook for 1 more hour, add a few drops of bottled hot sauce and serve.

◎ After the peas are done cooking, add 2 teaspoons chili powder and a can of chopped green chilies.

Orange-flavored Carrots

ingredients

3 cups fresh, sliced carrots

2 tablespoons onions chopped into small pieces

1/2 cup water

2 tablespoons of frozen orange juice (make juice with the rest!)

1 teaspoon lemon juice, fresh or bottled

1 Bring water in a medium-sized pot to a boil over high heat. Add the carrots, onion pieces, and salt and turn the heat down to medium.

2 Simmer until the carrots are tender, about 20 minutes.

3 Drain the mixture, but **save** 2 tablespoons of the cooking liquid. Put the carrots back into the pot.

4 Add the 2 tablespoons cooking liquid, the orange juice concentrate, and the lemon juice to the carrots. Stir gently. Heat over low heat until the carrots are warm.

HEY BABY, WE'RE GREAT TOGETHER!

Quick & Easy Raisin Pancake Squares

ingredients

1 egg

2 cups packaged pancake mix

1 1/2 cups milk

1/2 cup raisins

1 teaspoon cinnamon

2 tablespoons vegetable oil

Pancake toppings like syrup, honey, or jam

1 Turn oven on to 425°.

2 In a mixing bowl, combine milk, egg, and vegetable oil. Mix well.

3 Add the pancake mix and cinnamon. Stir to wet all the ingredients, but leave some lumps in it.

4 Stir in the raisins.

5 Coat a 9" x 13" baking pan with 1/2 teaspoon vegetable oil. Pour the batter into the pan and spread around evenly.

6 Bake for about 10 minutes, or until the edges are light brown.

7 Remove from the oven, cut into serving-sized squares, and serve with pancake toppings.

Maybe you don't like raisins...

Instead of raisins, you can add any of the following:

◎ 1/2 cup chopped dried apricots or peaches

◎ 1/2 cup chopped dried apples

◎ 1/3 cup small pieces of walnuts or pecans

◎ 1/3 cup quick-cooking oats (raw, not cooked)

Desserts

Renée's Best Chocolate Chip Cookies

ingredients

1/3 cup white sugar

1/2 cup brown sugar

1/2 cup (1 cube) butter, softened to room temperature *(to soften, either leave the butter, covered, at room temperature for an hour, or heat it in a microwave for 5 seconds)*

2 teaspoons vanilla extract

1 egg

1 1/2 cups flour

1/2 teaspoon baking soda

1/2 teaspoon salt

1 1/2 cups semi-sweet chocolate chips

1 Preheat oven to 350°.

2 In a mixing bowl combine the soft butter and the sugars. Beat with a spoon until it's smooth and creamy.

3 Stir in the egg and vanilla.

4 In a separate bowl mix together the flour, baking soda, and salt. Mix about half this mixture into the butter mixture. Add in the rest of the flour mixture and mix well. Stir in the chocolate chips.

5 Spoon small mounds of cookie dough onto an ungreased cookie sheet, about 2 inches apart. Bake 10 minutes. Remove from the oven and let cool for a few minutes. Remove cookies with a pancake turner and put them onto a wire cooling rack or a plate.

Brownies

ingredients

1/2 cup butter (1 stick) softened to room temperature *(to soften, either leave the butter, covered, at room temperature for an hour, or heat it in a microwave for 5 seconds)*

1 cup sugar

2 eggs

1/2 cup flour

1/4 cup unsweetened cocoa

1/2 teaspoon vegetable oil

1 Preheat oven to 350°.

2 In a mixing bowl combine the soft butter and the sugars. Beat with a spoon until it's smooth and creamy.

3 Stir in the eggs one at a time.

4 In another bowl combine the flour and cocoa together. Add this to the butter mixture. Mix thoroughly until smooth.

5 Smear the vegetable oil inside a 9"x9" pan. Pour in the brownie batter.

6 Bake at 350° for 20 minutes. Be careful not to overcook them or they will be dry instead of chewy. Remove them from the oven and let cool 20 minutes before cutting them into squares.

 This recipe is included in the Vegetarian Menu Plan (pg 20-21)

Choco-Peanut Butter Candy

ingredients

1/3 cup confectioners sugar *(finely powdered white sugar mixed with cornstarch—find it in the baking ingredients section of the grocery store, near the regular white sugar)*

2 tablespoons unsweetened cocoa

2 teaspoons water

2 teaspoons peanut butter

3 tablespoons confectioners sugar for coating candy

1 Combine the confectioners sugar with the cocoa in a small mixing bowl.

2 Mix in 2 teaspoons water, and stir until the sugar and cocoa make a smooth paste.

3 Add the peanut butter and mix until smooth.

4 Using your clean hands, form little balls (about 1" across). Roll each one in confectioners sugar so they're coated all over, then place on a plate. Store leftovers in the refrigerator.

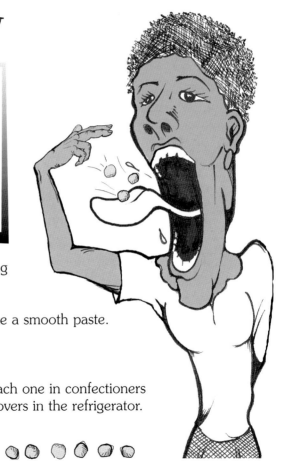

Pineapple Upside-down Cake

ingredients

1/3 cup butter, softened to room temperature (*to soften, either leave the butter, covered, at room temperature for an hour, or heat it in a microwave for 5 seconds*)

1/2 cup sugar

1/2 cup brown sugar

2 cups flour

2 teaspoons baking powder

1/4 teaspoon salt

2 eggs

1/2 cup milk

1 teaspoon vanilla extract

for the topping:

1 15-oz can diced pineapple

2 tablespoons butter

1 cup brown sugar

1 In a mixing bowl, mix together the butter and both sugars until smooth.

2 Mix in eggs one at a time.

3 Add the flour, baking powder, and salt. Mix well. Set the batter aside.

4 Place the 2 tablespoons butter in a 9"x9" pan, place the pan in the hot, preheated oven for 2 minutes, or until the butter melts.

This recipe is included in the 12th Street Menu Plan (pg 16-17)

5 Remove the pan and add 2/3 cup brown sugar. Stir with a spoon to combine the butter and brown sugar into a paste. Spread the paste evenly over the bottom of the pan.

6 Drain the liquid off the canned pineapple pieces. Spread them evenly over the top of the butter and sugar paste. Pour the batter over the top.

7 Bake at 350° for 45 minutes. Remove from the oven, let cool in the pan for at least 30 minutes. To serve, cut a piece of cake and turn it upside down on the plate so the pineapple is on top.

Peaches and Cream

Invite your friends over—this makes enough for 2 to 3 people.

ingredients

1 15-oz can peaches, cut into pieces (you can buy them already cut up)

1 teaspoon cinnamon

2/3 cup baking mix (like Bisquick, for example)

2 eggs

1 tablespoon vegetable oil

1/2 cup sugar

1 Preheat oven to 375°.

2 Drain all the liquid off the canned peaches. Cut them into bite-sized pieces. Place the pieces evenly over the bottom of a 9"x9" baking pan.

3 In a mixing bowl combine the baking mix, eggs, oil, and sugar. Mix until smooth. Pour batter over the peaches in the pan.

4 Bake at 375° for 40-45 minutes, or until a knife inserted in the middle comes out without any batter stuck to it. Serve plain or with whipped cream.

Feeling adventurous?

Try using either canned apricots or cherries instead of the peaches.

 This recipe is included in the Vegetarian Menu Plan (pg 20-21)

Apple Crisp

ingredients

6 apples	1/2 cup oatmeal
2 tablespoons sugar	1/2 cup flour
1 teaspoon cinnamon	1/2 cup butter
3/4 cup brown sugar	

1 Cut apples into wedges, peel off skin, then cut out the core. Cut the peeled wedges into bite-sized chunks.

2 Place apples in a mixing bowl.

3 Add the sugar and cinnamon to the apples and stir to coat evenly. Put apples in a 9"x9" pan.

4 Preheat oven to 350°.

5 Melt the butter either in a bowl in the microwave on high for 20 seconds, or on the stove in small pot on low heat.

6 In the mixing bowl that had the apples in it, combine the oatmeal, flour, and melted butter. Spread this mixture evenly over the apple pieces in the pan.

7 Bake at 350° for 45 minutes, or until the apples are soft and the top is lightly browned on the edges.

This recipe is included in the Southwestern Style Menu Plan (pg 24-25)

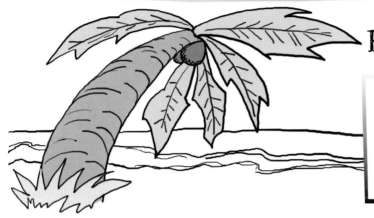

Fried Bananas

ingredients

1 banana, firm and yellow

2 tablespoons butter

2 teaspoons lemon juice or lime juice

1 tablespoon honey

1 Cut a lemon or lime in half and squeeze out 2 teaspoons of juice into a small bowl. Set aside.

2 Peel the banana and cut it in half lengthwise (from tip to tip), then cut each half in half crosswise. Now you have 4 pieces of banana.

3 In a frying pan, add the butter and turn heat to medium. As soon as the butter melts increase the heat to medium high and add the bananas.

4 Fry them quickly on 1 side until lightly browned, then turn over with a pancake turner and fry quickly on the second side until lightly browned. It should take about 2 minutes total.

5 Remove bananas to a bowl. Immediately spoon the lemon juice over the bananas, then drizzle them with the honey. Serve plain or with vanilla ice cream.

 This recipe is included in the 12th Street Menu Plan (pg 16-17)

What's a Food Pyramid?

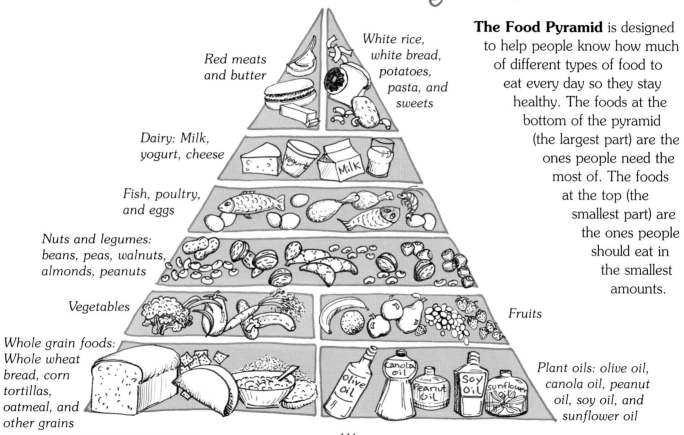

Red meats and butter

White rice, white bread, potatoes, pasta, and sweets

Dairy: Milk, yogurt, cheese

Fish, poultry, and eggs

Nuts and legumes: beans, peas, walnuts, almonds, peanuts

Vegetables

Fruits

Whole grain foods: Whole wheat bread, corn tortillas, oatmeal, and other grains

Plant oils: olive oil, canola oil, peanut oil, soy oil, and sunflower oil

The Food Pyramid is designed to help people know how much of different types of food to eat every day so they stay healthy. The foods at the bottom of the pyramid (the largest part) are the ones people need the most of. The foods at the top (the smallest part) are the ones people should eat in the smallest amounts.

How do meals fit into the Food Pyramid?

Each meal you eat is made up of foods from the different food groups in the pyramid.

Here is how a serving of **Tuna Noodle Casserole** fits into the food pyramid.

1 serving of
Tuna Noodle Casserole
(*see recipe on pg 41*):

noodles (Pasta)

mozzarella cheese
(Dairy)

milk (Dairy)

tuna fish (Fish)

green beans (Vegetables)

condensed cream of
mushroom soup (Plant
Oils *and* Vegetables)

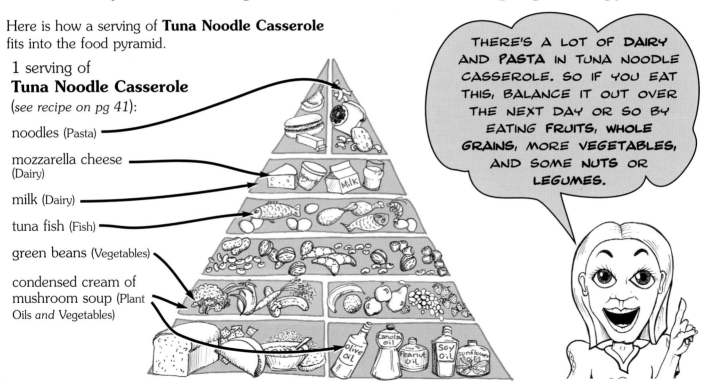

THERE'S A LOT OF **DAIRY** AND **PASTA** IN TUNA NOODLE CASSEROLE. SO IF YOU EAT THIS, BALANCE IT OUT OVER THE NEXT DAY OR SO BY EATING FRUITS, WHOLE GRAINS, MORE VEGETABLES, AND SOME NUTS OR LEGUMES.

Even meals you buy can be divided into the Pyramid food groups.

Here is how a serving of **Double Cheeseburger and Fries** fits into the food pyramid:

Double Cheeseburger and Fries
(*the kind you can buy at fast-food restaurants*):

French fries (Potatoes)

Hamburger bun
(White Bread)

Beef (Red Meat)

Cheese (Dairy)

Mayonnaise (Eggs and Plant Oils)

Pickle slices (tiny amount of Vegetables)

Lettuce (Vegetables)

Ketchup

Mustard

A BURGER AND FRIES HAS LOTS OF **WHITE BREAD, POTATOES,** AND **RED MEAT** FROM THE TOP OF THE PYRAMID. THE DAY I ATE THIS MEAL, I BALANCED IT OUT BY EATING **FRUITS, VEGETABLES, WHOLE GRAINS, MILK,** AND **BEANS** AT OTHER MEALS.

Index

Notes

Notes

National Edition, Vol. 17, No. 1

December, 2004

Getting Ready®

A RESOURCE FOR INDEPEN... ...VING

THERE'S A WAY OUT!

Dark Days
Finding a way out of depression

Getting Ready

The monthly magazine jam-packed with information on life skills!

Teens listen to what other teens have to say, right?

That's why you'll love reading *Getting Ready's* compelling first-person stories by struggling teens in care. Created to grab attention and spark conversation, *Getting Ready* offers interesting stories, entertaining cartoons, and photo essays that show you what you need to know for living on your own.

Each issue covers topics such as:

- jobs
- housing
- legal issues
- money management
- health
- & much more...

Subscribe to Getting Ready magazine!
ph: 800.777.6636 or 541.343.6636
email: nwm@northwestmedia.com

Go to www.SocialLearning.com for more resources on life skills.